THE ROUNDHOUSE VOICES

Books by Dave Smith

POETRY

Gray Soldiers
In the House of the Judge
Homage to Edgar Allan Poe
Dream Flights
Goshawk, Antelope
Cumberland Station
The Fisherman's Whore
Mean Rufus Throw Down

LIMITED EDITIONS

Blue Spruce
In Dark, Sudden with Light
Drunks
Bull Island

CRITICISM

Local Assays
The Pure Clear Word: Essays on the Poetry of James Wright

FICTION

Onliness
Southern Delights

ANTHOLOGIES

The Morrow Anthology of Younger American Poets (*editor*)

THE ROUNDHOUSE VOICES

SELECTED AND NEW POEMS

DAVE SMITH

PERENNIAL LIBRARY

Harper & Row, Publishers, New York
Cambridge, Philadelphia, San Francisco, London
Mexico City, São Paulo, Singapore, Sydney

This book is dedicated with love to
DEE SMITH

Copyright acknowledgments appear on page 183.

THE ROUNDHOUSE VOICES: SELECTED AND NEW POEMS. Copyright © 1985 by
Dave Smith. All rights reserved. Printed in the United States of America. No part
of this book may be used or reproduced in any manner whatsoever without
written permission except in the case of brief quotations embodied in critical
articles and reviews. For information address Harper & Row, Publishers, Inc.,
10 East 53rd Street, New York, N.Y. 10022. Published simultaneously in Canada
by Fitzhenry & Whiteside Limited, Toronto.

FIRST EDITION

Designer: Sidney Feinberg

Library of Congress Cataloging in Publication Data

Smith, Dave, 1942–
   The roundhouse voices.

   "Perennial library"
   I. Title.
PS3569.M5173R6   1985   811'.54   83-48804
   ISBN 0-06-015473-X   85 86 87 88 89   RRD 10 9 8 7 6 5 4 3 2 1
   ISBN 0-06-096007-8 (pbk.) 85 86 87 88 89   RRD 10 9 8 7 6 5 4 3 2 1

Contents

THE ROUNDHOUSE VOICES

The Roundhouse Voices

In full glare of sunlight I came here, man-tall but thin
as a pinstripe, and stood outside the rusted fence
with its crown of iron thorns while
the soot cut into our lungs with tiny diamonds.
I walked through houses with my grain-lovely slugger
from Louisville that my uncle bought and stood
in the sun that made its glove soft on my hand
until I saw my chance to crawl under and get past
anyone who would demand a badge and a name.

The guard hollered that I could get the hell from there quick
when I popped in his face like a thief. All I ever wanted
to steal was life and you can't get that easy
in the grind of a railyard. *You can't catch me,
lardass, I can go left or right good as the Mick,*
I hummed to him, holding my slugger by the neck
for a bunt laid smooth where the coal cars
jerked and let me pass between tracks
until, in a slide on ash, I fell safe and heard
the wheeze of his words: *Who the hell are you, kid?*

I hear them again tonight, Uncle, hard as big brakeshoes,
when I lean over your face in the box of silk. The years
you spent hobbling from room to room alone crawl
up my legs and turn this house to another
house, round and black as defeat, where slugging
comes easy when you whip the gray softball over
the glass diesel globe. Footsteps thump on the stairs
like that fat ball against bricks and when I miss
I hear you warn me to watch the timing, to keep
my eyes on your hand and forget the fence,

hearing also that other voice that keeps me out and away
from you on a day worth playing good ball. Hearing
Who the hell . . . I see myself like a burning speck

3

of cinder come down the hill and through a tunnel
of porches like stands, running on deep ash,
and I give him the finger, whose face still gleams
clear as a B&O headlight, just to make him get up
and chase me into a dream of scoring at your feet.
At Christmas that guard staggered home sobbing,
the thing in his chest tight as a torque wrench.
In the summer I did not have to run and now

who is the one who dreams of a drink as he leans over
tools you kept bright as a first-girl's promise? I
have no one to run from or to, nobody to give
my finger to as I steal his peace. Uncle, the light
bleeds on your gray face like the high barbed-wire
shadows I had to get through and maybe you don't remember
you said to come back, to wait and you'd show me
the right way to take a hard pitch
in the sun that shudders on the ready man. I'm here

though this is a day I did not want to see. In the roundhouse
the rasp and heel-click of compressors is still,
soot lies deep in every greasy fingerprint.
I called you from the pits and you did not come up
and I felt the fear when I stood on the tracks
that are like stars which never lead us
into any kind of light and I don't know who'll
tell me now when the guard sticks his blind snoot
between us: take off and beat the bastard out.
Can you hear him over the yard, grabbing his chest,
cry out, *Who the goddamn hell are you, kid?*

I gave him every name in the book, Uncle, but he caught us
and what good did all those hours of coaching do?
You lie on your back, eyeless forever, and I think
how once I climbed to the top of a diesel and stared
into that gray roundhouse glass where, in anger,
you threw up the ball and made a star
to swear at greater than the Mick ever dreamed.
It has been years but now I know what followed there
every morning the sun came up, not light
but the puffing bad-bellied light of words.

All day I have held your hand, trying to say back that life,
to get under that fence with words I lined
and linked up and steamed into a cold room
where the illusion of hope means skin torn in boxes
of tools. The footsteps come pounding into words
and even the finger I give death is words
that won't let us be what we wanted, each one
chasing and being chased by dreams in the dark.
Words are all we ever were and they did us
no damn good. Do you hear that?

Do you hear the words that, in oiled gravel, you gave me
when you set my feet in the right stance to swing?
They are coal-hard and they come in wings
and loops like despair not even the Mick
could knock out of this room, words softer
than the centers of hearts in guards or uncles,
words skinned and numbed by too many bricks.
I have had enough of them and bring them back here
where the tick and creak of everything dies
in your tiny starlight and I stand down
on my knees to cry, *Who the hell are you, kid?*

SELECTED POEMS

Quick as the waves breaking under an east wind,
Dark as the winter-browed sea-sky,
The crowd of memories waking in the heart—
                    —Venantius Fortunatus

Near the Docks

There was a fire in the night.
Across the street I slept among the others
as the ashes snowed upon small pines.
I slept owning nothing, a child ignorant
of fortune's blistering story, the playful
flash in the dark, the unseen smolder
that would leave us revealed, unchanged.
I said my prayers for luck
but the man trying to live in two houses
answers me now, losing
neither the old one whose windows burst
with weariness, nor the one half-built
whose roofless, green timbers
he would leave unfinished like a vision.
I had climbed there all summer to smoke.

Awake, I found him sitting at his stool
halfway between the houses
where I would go each morning. The story
of the sea would be upon his tongue,
his hands weaving the wire to a trap,
making the careful seams to catch
a scuttling crab. Beyond him, his wife
already had begun to stretch her wash,
indifferent in that early light, and a dog
lapped from the ruts of the fire truck.

I believed little had been changed by fire,
only his toolshed limp as a black sail
left in a heap, and a new hole
in the landscape. This was an old place
where no one came, luckless, desperate,
eternal as guilt. In silence
I greeted that old one. But now I remember

seeing also, as if for the first time,
the shocking gray face of the sea.
It loomed up human and beautiful
as far off the figures of boats crossed,
worked, and seemed to sink
while they burned in the sullen sun.

Among the Oyster Boats at Plum Tree Cove

I have been away growing old
at the heart of another country
where there are no boats crumbling,
or small crabs with scuttling tools.
These pines warped with early snow,
this light that slopes and breaks
as the sea slides, sloughing
against your air and earth-worn
flanks: I had loosed the dead
from memory but, coming back
confused, I find them waiting
here at the sea's rattling edge.

It is too much to speak to them, yet
to them through you I bow, politely
soiled and whiskered, wanting to drink,
to stand under the old harsh throats
sharing whiskey at Plum Tree, among
the booted ones with plaid shirts
and large loving hands. But wanting
is not enough; you only groan or
roll and the village sleeps off
its wild hours among neat azaleas.
I stand among you tasting silence
as the wind softly licks the wave.

The Shark in the Rafters

Under the stuttered snatch of the winch
they draw him by pulley and wheel,
the net-fouler unaccountably caught.
Slower than the night tracking
the sun through warm furrows
he rises into the open fishhouse
where the sea flicks womb-blue
at a hole hacked in the house floor.

It is not this mechanical shriek but one
like that of a reed blown on in the palm
that reaches the women, brings them
out of the darkness of pine needles
and laboring in labyrinths of swampgrass
where age-ruptured boats lie buried.

Some come as widows and some as children,
all bluntly gazing like lovers,
to stand before this last house at the point.
Here are no windows and no doors,
only the tin roof with the tallest fire
of the sun and a mild iron-headed
animal swaying like a wing in the air.

Possessed by his timber-shaking shadow,
mouths red as gill slits, they whisper
he is beautiful and terrible, terrible,
as they jam the steel bars inside
the silken jaws, spooning, hooking
free the stump of a man's leg until
a shape sliced from malice and fear
comes hard to each face in the blaze.

With blood-sluice flowing from the house
over the minnow-seeded smile of water,
each of the women leans close as if
to pass beyond the passionless wall
of light a finger's single, forbidden
touch at the hide that has entered
all space between the eyes and the sun.

Even the children hidden in old hulls
grow still remembering what they have
heard of holes huge in the nets
as the shadow is halved by the head
of the roof, cranked up to wait
where a young man has climbed, his
knife winking flashes of promise
over the heads of girls in the surf.

Then one by one the gore-teeth are made
astonishingly large, the eyes gouged,
tossed to the swarm of minnows,
the flesh peeled out in tongues, coiled
entrails slipped free like ribbons,
the baby bones shone into the room
of brass-flaring glare, until only
the heart remains. Now the men cry,
hammer-headed grunts, and the dark meat
floats out slick from hand to hand

to be hacked in many parts and heaved
through the floor where the tide turns
far off with the moon in desire.
At the feet of women the gobbets
bloodied and sparkling ride up, bob,
and sink to the ooze of mud while
the man who had risen for them
looms down with his knife, flesh-
flecked, birth-bloody in descent.

And this afternoon, children abandoned
in the playful plunge of their bodies,
turning to the reed-rustle of night

the daughters of daughters will rise
to remember how an unwedded woman hangs
above a sea-splintered floor, lies
with a swimmer's shadow upon her
where a clock ticks and whispers.
The clock's face will be luminous
in the waves of darkness, erect
hands white, sheer as the teeth
that hide until known once.
Speaking of death, they will
begin with the heart so easily adrift
in pieces, the salt mouth hugely open.

Rooster Smith's Last Log Canoe

—at the Mariner's Museum, Newport News, Virginia

Suspended in a vast pendulum of blue light
they keep alive the legends of boats,
the whole evolution of their making

huddled beneath the giant bust
of an American Eagle
whose wings filter the sun, whose

talons press and hold a huge brass dial
which spreads time on the floor
like moss in a cove.

Each step drops a man deeper in the Eagle's
eye, and there is one room Rooster
lives in, a man recognizable

by the scars on his hand or the shy
shadowy way he poses by his last boat,
as if he is saying again and again

this one is for you, this I have well built.
His arm bends into the curved bow
and the chines of heartwood.

On that wall there is a series of photographs
as precise and stiff as half-inch
sheets of James River ice.

In the first, a tree, fully leafed, rippled
sunshine on the slack water in the rear.
Nothing else has happened.

Rooster stands then by the corpse of an ancient
trunk, his saw baring its teeth like a fish.
He seems sad or winded.

Two men, one shadowed and grim, one lighter, lean
into the hollowed body of wood, their faces
turned up, surprised. Here, the river ribbons flat.

A keel rises in the bladed reeds. Ribs glisten.
The men lean on each other; wood chips
fleck the gray earth like stars.

A mast leads the eye to the center of the river
where specks seem loose, errant, whipped
by wind's domination. No men appear.

On Model-A wheels, she strains at the edge
of Deep Creek Point. Pines like massive wings
hover over the hull. Rooster looks

to the next photograph, where she is under way.
He is missing, and the other man.
It is marked THE LAST BAY CANOE.

Under the final frame, the green hull sleeps
in its chocks, a tree full of warm light,
its body groaning for water. Your hand,

which once swung from Rooster's calloused fingers,
presses the chines to feel where blade,
fire, sweat made their marks.

Some things do not show in two-dimensional gloss:
pain in the chest, arm-breaking knots.
Northeast storms escape this room.

But with the hand speaking to the wood, under
the Eagle's time-splintering gaze,
a wind in a wind begins to blow.

You listen the way a child does, feeling
in the open chinks and caulkless seams
for Rooster's empty bottles.

Everything is exactly right, the dark stain
on the stern seat, the heavy chain links
played out, the bird circling overhead.

In that dusk-deflected light you are told
your grandmother's torn skirt still remains,
a piece of the sea's tongue in wood's belly.

The Spinning Wheel in the Attic

Not for beauty's sake, or art's, this wheel
   came round in his calloused palms,
      bent willows and oak,

formed for the work of spinning whole cloth,
   gatherer of scraps fine and coarse,
      a tool. Shuttle and stroke,

long nights he labored in the ways of stars.
   His back bowed with shafts of steel
      hewing wheel and spoke

from the supple wood hardening him to a fist.
   No consideration of death's awl, no
      fear of time's trap

led him to lay on signature or sign. He finished
   undeceived by the things he made.
      He wore a plain hat.

I can see his whittle marks as faint as scars,
   and edges he'd fail to sand
      when he fretted at

the grain's refusal to have his slightest urge.
   My finger drawn in years of dust
      shows the wood raw,

stained by sweat or blood, the secret knots
   clear now as wire buried in a limb
      that buckles the saw

into the flesh so a man will curse what he needs
   but bend in whatever weather to work,
      licking lips, clamping jaw

while at window the woman, still, watches him.
    Sometimes he imagines what she will
        weave, not the coverlet

she'll die under, cold on their bed, never that,
    that will rise from homespun thread
        from the crop he's planted

to feed the sheep he'll shear, the dirty skeins
    stinking on the floor. But the touch
        of beauty is her gift,

he thinks. She has no illusions. This is her work
    only: making a family cloth to keep
        off cold and harm. Wood

must serve, and serves to show glistening grooves
    where she drew together the threads,
        the seams, at times would

whimper in pain. But mostly sing. Think of him
    leaving this wheel in dark air, touching
        her cloth, the last good

shove returning it all in a single spooling instant,
    love's first star-groan, the plow-peeled
        tang of earth, her spine

sparking in hearthlight, spinning for babies, deaths,
    until it stood without use, a shadow he'd
        bang against, surprised

by his pain, then listening as it sang easily alone,
    beyond purpose or understanding, a voice
        out of the void, alive.

On a Field Trip at Fredericksburg

The big steel tourist shield says maybe
fifteen thousand got it here. No word
of either Whitman or one uncle
I barely remember in the smoke
that filled his tiny mountain house.

If each finger were a thousand of them
I could clap my hands and be dead
up to my wrists. It was quick
though not so fast as we can do it
now, one bomb, atomic or worse,
the tiny pod slung on wingtip,
high up, an egg cradled
by some rapacious mockingbird.

Hiroshima canned nine times their number
in a flash. Few had the time
to moan or feel the feeling
ooze back in the groin.

In a ditch I stand
above Marye's Heights, the book-
bred faces of Brady's fifteen-year-old
drummers, before battle, rigid
as August's dandelions
all the way to the Potomac
rolling in my skull.

If Audubon came here, the names
of birds would gush, the marvel
single feathers make
evoke a cloud, a nation,
a gray blur preserved
on a blue horizon, but

there is only a wandering child,
one dark stalk snapped off
in her hand. Hopeless teacher,
I take it, try to help her
hold its obscure syllables
one instant in her mouth,
like a drift of wind
at the forehead, the front door,
the black, numb fingernails.

How to Get to Green Springs

Nobody knows exactly when it fell off the map
or what the pressures were on its flooding river.
The hedge, the tottering mailbox, were gone. That dimple
of light from the bicycle that raised itself to creak
at noon across a clattering bridge names my father.
His blood silent as a surging wish drags this town
lost through my body, a place I can get back to only
by hunch and a train whistle that was right on time.

But time and trains were never right in Green Springs,
West Virginia. What color could map the coal's grime,
shacks shored against the river every March, mail
left to rot because no one answered to occupant?
Farmers low on sugar cursed the heat and left bad cigars
boys would puff back to clouds where they dreamed
of girls naked as their hands under outfield flies.
Scores were low. There were no springs for the sick.
Women lined their walls with the Sears catalog, but
the only fur they ever had was a warbled rabbit.
To get here think of dirt, think of night leaking,
the tick of waterbugs, a train held in Pittsburgh.

Cumberland Station

Gray brick, ash, hand-bent railings, steps so big
it takes hours to mount them, polished oak
pews holding the slim hafts of sun, and one
splash of the *Pittsburgh Post-Gazette*. The man
who left Cumberland gone, come back, no job
anywhere. I come here alone, shaken
the way I came years ago to ride down
mountains in Big Daddy's cab. He was
the first set cold in the black meadow.

Six rows of track gleam, thinned, rippling
like water on walls where famous engines steam, half
submerged in frothing crowds with something
to celebrate and plenty to eat. One engineer takes
children for a free ride, a frolic
like an earthquake. Ash cakes their hair.
I am one of those who walked uphill
through flowers of soot to zing
scared to death into the world.

Now whole families afoot cruise South Cumberland
for something to do, no jobs, no money for bars,
the old stories cracked like wallets.
This time there's no fun in coming back. The second
death. My roundhouse uncle coughed his youth
into a gutter. His son, the third, slid on the ice,
losing his need to drink himself
stupidly dead. In this vaulted hall
I think of all the dirt poured down
from shovels and trains and empty pockets.
I stare into the huge malignant headlamps
circling the gray walls and catch a stuttered
glimpse of faces stunned like deer on a track,
children getting drunk, shiny as Depression apples.

Churning through the inner space of this godforsaken
wayside, I feel the ground try to upchuck and I dig
my fingers in my temples to bury a child
diced on a cowcatcher, a woman smelling
alkaline from washing out the soot.
Where I stood in that hopeless, hateful room
will not leave me. The scarf of smoke I saw
over a man's shoulder runs through me
like the sored Potomac River.

Grandfather, you ask why I don't visit you
now you have escaped the ticket-seller's cage
to fumble hooks and clean the Shakespeare reels.
What could we catch? I've been sitting in the pews
thinking about us a long time, long enough to see
a man can't live in jobless, friendless Cumberland
anymore. The soot owns even the fish.

I keep promising I'll come back, we'll get out,
you and me, like brothers, and I mean it.
A while ago a man with the look of a demented cousin
shuffled across this skittery floor and snatched up
the *Post-Gazette* and stuffed it in his coat
and nobody gave a damn because nobody cares
who comes or goes here or even who steals
what nobody wants: old news, photographs
of dead diesels behind chipped glass.

I'm the man who stole it and I wish you were here
to beat the hell out of me for it because
what you said a long time ago welts my face
and won't go away. I admit
it isn't mine even if it's nobody else's.
Anyway, that's all I catch this trip—bad
news. I can't catch my nephew's life, my uncle's,
Big Daddy's, yours, or the ash-haired kids'
who fell down to sleep here after the war.

Outside new families pick their way along tracks
you and I have walked home on many nights.

Every face on the walls goes on smiling,
and, Grandfather, I wish I had the guts
to tell you this is a place I hope
I never have to go through again.

The Spring Poem

Everyone should write a Spring poem
—Louise Glück

Yes, but we must be sure of verities
such as proper heat and adequate form.
That's what poets are for, is my theory.
This then is a Spring poem. A car warms
its rusting hulk in a meadow; weeds slog
up its flanks in martial weather. April
or late March is our month. There is a fog
of spunky mildew and sweaty tufts spill
from the damp rump of a back seat. A spring
thrusts one gleaming tip out, a brilliant tooth
uncoiling from Winter's tension, a ring
of insects along, working out the Truth.
Each year this car, melting around that spring,
hears nails trench from boards and every squeak sing.

Boats

1. *On the Poquoson River*

Rounding a slip of the marsh, the boat skids
under me and the propeller whines naked,
then digs and shoots me forward. A clapper rail
disappears in reeds and one crane, shaken
from his nap, blinks and holds.

He makes me think of the Lost Tribe of Virginia,
as if the scree of insects was the Jew's
harp in John Jacob Niles's mouth.

A creek opens its throat and I enter, dragging
down to hear my wake's slip-slop,
thinking of the man who warned me people
were the same everywhere, lost and wondering

how they came to the life no one else wanted.
Sweet Jesus, he was right. Now he lies
in this sodden ground for the first time
in his life and I do not know even where.

Today is no different, the waters flood hulks
of empty houses, leaving beer cans to gleam
under the grinding moon. The first stalks
of narcissus break the ground with gold
though March still means tonight to freeze.

I know this place, its small mustering of facts
wind-worn and useless, real and repeated, the same
anywhere. At the end the creek leads to a room,
one placid boat swinging at a stick, pines sieving

air, the cleat ringing like small jewelry.

2. *The Cunner in the Calotype*

You need to know these boats, cunners, square
of bow and stern, never painted, always with a bottle
floating where the bilge is always rank and deep.
Sometimes they hold the sun like a butter tub but
nobody ever stepped a sail in one. They're used
to ferry out to where oyster scows squat, sere
and long as a lovely woman's thigh in an old dream.
You need to ask why they lie cracked, sucking salt
water through the reed tubes, what has happened
to shove them back into the center of the marsh
where the scree of gnats goes out when a fisherman,
desperate in the end, shoves his finger in his ear.
You need to hear the slow toll of rope-ends, mossed
like drifting arms, the bell-cry of cleat and chained
transom stained a hundred hues by years of seas.

When the dozers come to take the marsh, slapping down
layers of asphalt, when the all-temperature malls rise,
when women of the garden club cease their designing,
cunners will be gone, claimed by antique freaks, smashed
for scrap, the creeks leveled, the sun deceived with
only absence flashing in the heat. They're unemployed,
no swimming boys will sink them for a joke, no wind
whip and toss them in a storm or leave them in a tree.
The fishermen exchange their daily poverty for jobs
behind counters; few men ever rowed a boat on dirt.
What you'd get for one wouldn't pay for a week's beer.
It is for them, fathers you need to know, I give you
this cunner of my place, its hand-hacked bottom whole
still, smell of crabs yet rank here, a man's hat
floating in the black water as if mislaid, going down.

Sailing the Back River

Tonight no one takes fish. Tattered pennants
of T-shirts flap, their shadows riding wave crests,
among the hulls half-ashore and wholly sunken.
Always I am the waterman snagging nets on keels
in the graveyard of boats, the pale sailor who
glides with the music of nails through plank rot
and oil scum to sit in the toy wheelhouse of fathers.

I do not ask you to come with me or even to watch
the pennants signaling the drift of the winds.
Nothing I could do would raise one body bound
under these mud-struck beams, but I mean to do
what I can to save my own waterlogged life and here
is the best place I know to beg. I throw out love
like an anchor and wait where the long houselights
of strangers tickle the river's back. I go alone

as a creaky-boned woman goes to the far bench
at the heart of her garden where the rose suffers.
There will be time for you to hold in your palm
what each has held here, the sudden canting of gulls,
a room with one back-broken chair, the potbelly
sputtering as it answers the wind, the soft knock
waters make at the fair skin of roots. I come here
to stop up my lying words: your life was always bad.

Isn't it right to drag the rivers for the bodies
not even the nets could catch? I won't lie, I want
you to lie with me on the tumbling surface of love.
This is the place to honor crab song, reed's aria,
where every hour the mussel sighs *begin again*. Say
I am water and learn what I hold as river, creek,
lake, ditch or sewer. I am equal with fire and ice.
We are one body sailing or nothing. My life, yours,
what are they but hulls homing, moving the sand?

The Perspective & Limits of Snapshots

Aubrey Bodine's crosswater shot of Menchville,
Virginia: a little dream composing a little water,
specifically, the Deep Creek flank of the James.
Two-man oyster scows lie shoulder to shoulder,
as if you walk them, one land to another,
no narrow channel hidden in the glossy middle
like a blurred stroke, current grinning at hulls.
It is an entirely eloquent peace, with lolling
ropes and liquid glitter, this vision of traffic
and no oystermen in sight. Clearly, Bodine is not
Mathew Brady catching the trenchant gropes frozen
at Fredericksburg with a small black box. So well
has he excluded the neat Mennonite church, yachts,
country club pool, the spare smell of dignity seeps.
Perhaps it is because of the zoom on the teeth
of the oyster tongs; perhaps it is after all Sunday.

Above the last boat, the flat-faced store squats
at the end of the dirt road as if musing over
accounts receivable. No doubt it has weathered
years of blood spilling. A spotted hound lifts
his nose above what must be yesterday's trash fish,
his white coat luminous against deep foliage. What
Bodine fails to see is the dog turning to lope
uphill under that screen of poplars, behind fat
azaleas that hide the country farm and the drunks
pressed against wire screens, sniffing the James.
One oysterman thumped his noisy wife (the window
was accidental) because she had a knife and mourned
their boy twenty years drowned. If he knew Bodine
stood at the marsh tip where his boy dove, if he
were but told a camera yawned to suck in the years

of his worst sailing shame, he would turn away. He
would whistle up boys in the dust that is dignity
and if he could he would spit in his hand and tell
his nameless black cellmate there are many men
for whom the world is neither oyster nor pearl.

Night Fishing for Blues

At Fortress Monroe, Virginia,
the big-jawed Bluefish, ravenous, sleek muscle slamming
at rock, at pier legs, drives into Chesapeake
shallows, convoys rank after rank,
        wheeling through flume and flute of blood,
        something like hunger's throb hooking
until you hear it and know them there,
                            the family.
        Tonight, not far from where Jefferson Davis

hunched in a harrowing cell, gray eyes quick
as crabs' nubs, I come back over planks
deep drummed under boots years ago, tufts of hair

floating at my eyes, thinking it is right now
        to pitch through tideturn and mudslur
        for fish with teeth like snapped sabers.
        In blue crescents of base lights, I cast hooks

baited with Smithfield ham: they reel, zing,
plummet, coil in corrosive swirls, bump on
scum-skinned rocks. No skin divers prowl here,

        visibility an arm's length, my visions

hand-to-hand in the line's warp. A meat-
baited lure limps through limbs nippling the muck,
silhouettes, shoots forward, catches a cruising Blue

        sentry's eye, snags and sets

case-hardened barbs. Suddenly, I am not alone:
        three Negroes plump down in lawn chairs, shudder-
        casting into the black pod plodding under us. One

        ripples with age, a grandmotherly obelisk,

her breath puffing like a coal stove. She swivels
heavily, chewing her dark nut, spits thick juice
like a careful chum.

          When I yank the first Blue
she mumbles, her eyes roll far out on the black-
blue billowing sea-screen. I hear her canting

     to Africa, a cluck in her throat, a chain

song from the fisherman's house. I cannot
understand. Bluefish are pouring at me in squads.
I haul two, three at a time, torpedoes, moon-shiners,
jamming my feet into the splintered floor, battling
whatever comes. I know I have waited
a whole life for this minute. Like dreams

     graven on cold cell walls, Blues walk over

our heads, ground on back-wings, grind their teeth.
They splash rings of blue and silver around us, tiaras
of lost battalions. I can smell the salt of ocean
runners as she hollers *I ain't doing so bad
for an old queen.* No time to answer. Two

     car-hoods down her descendants swing sinewy arms

in Superfly shirts, exotic butterflies: I hear them
pop beer cans, the whoosh released like stale breath
through a noose no one remembers. We hang

     fast flat casts, artless, no teasing fishermen,

beyond the book-bred lures of the pristine streams,
speeded-up, centrifugal, machines wound
too far, belts slipped, gears gone, momentum

     hauling us back, slinging lines, winging wildly

as howitzers. Incredibly it happens: I feel
the hook hammer and shake and throw my entire weight
to dragging, as if I have caught the goddamndest

    Blue in the Atlantic. She screams: *Oh my God!*

Four of us fumbling in beamed headlight and blue
arc light cut the hook from her face. Gnats butterfly,
nag us: I put it deep and it must be gouged out
like a cyst. When it is free, I hear Blues not yet

    dead flopping softly. I tell her it is a lucky
    thing she can see. She mops blood blued over
    gold-lined teeth and opens her arms so her dress

    billows like a caftan. She wants

nothing but to fish. I hand her her pole, then cast
as far as I can. She pumps, wings a sinker and hooks
into flashing slop and reels hard. In one instant both

    our lines leap rigid as daguerreotypes; we have

caught each other but we go on for the blue blood of
ghosts that thrash in the brain's empty room.
We pull at shadows until we see there is nothing, then
sit on the shaky pier like prisoners. Coil after coil
we trace the path of Bluefish-knots backward,

    unlooping, feeling for holes, giving, testing,

slapping the gnats from our skins. Harried, unbound,
we leap to be fishers. But now a gray glow
shreds with the cloud curtain, an old belly-fire

    guts the night. Already the tide humps around

on itself. Lights flicker like campfires in duty windows
at Fort Monroe. She hooks up, saying *Sons they done
let us go.* I cast once more but nothing bites. Everywhere

      a circle of Blues bleaches, stiffens

in flecks of blood. We kneel, stuff styrofoam
boxes with blankets of ice, break their backs
to keep them cold and sweet, the woman gravely
showing us what to do. By dawn the stink has passed

      out of our noses. We drink beer like family.

All the way home thousands of Blues fall from my head,
falling with the gray Atlantic, and a pale veiny light
fills the road with sea-shadows that drift in figure

      eights, knot and snarl and draw me forward.

Messenger

It was not kindness, but I was only buckle-high in the door.
I let him in because the knock had come, the rain
clawed each window and wall. I was afraid.
Climbing down the stairs I did not know
how my country, cunningly, had rotted,
but hear, now, my steps creak in memory
and the rocks let go in the blind nightglass
where you get up, frightened, to reenact
the irrational logic of flesh.

Even now I can't see why it happens, the moment of change,
but must try to witness each particular index
of landscape and irony of promise. I know
I was a child when the banging began, sleepless
with every light in the house blazing. Then
the man whose speech entangled me came in
from the mud-world. He could not
put together the clear words of hope
we dream, only the surge of a river.
He, who said it wasn't a fit thing

for anyone, half-grown, to have to imagine in this godforsaken
life, said there was a message, the river high,
no chance. I remember the wind at that door
breaking like a father's hand on my face.
Such hurting does not cease and maybe
that is why the man went on fumbling
for love, for the loving words
that might be knowledge. He gave me

this message. I took it, and took, without warning, grief's
language that piece by piece has shown me how
to connect dreamed moments skidding like rocks
in the silence of a Wyoming midnight.

Each of his rainy words, fragments
of the old sickness, passed into me,
then he was gone, miserable and emptied,
and I had no home but the heart's hut,
the blistering walls of loneliness,
the world's blue skymiles of longing.

Common with drowned fir and uncoiling crocus, then, I
walked in ignorance and entered this terrible life
that was always a dream of the future
in the relentless unsleep of those
who cannot remember the last thing they wanted
to say: that love exists. And in darkness
you have dreamed me into your world
with their message, their words
whispering an hour before black, sudden knocking

that, even as I recall it, begins in your heart's meat
to reverberate, oh, its noise is going
to wake you like a dove's desire.
This is the dream of the soft buckling
of flesh, the beautiful last erosions,
and I swear I would give up these words
if I could, I would stop the code
of that streetlight just beyond your bed—

but it is too late, for the secret of hope swells in you
and who can stop the news that already screams
like the roof's edge leaving its nails
over your child's bed that is, now,
splintered and empty as every moment
skidding at the back of your neck? Leaves
not a month old hurl out of the storm
and steady splatter of time, and tomorrow
will lie still ripening, but only long enough
for you to catalog, in dream, what was possible

before the rake must drag its scritch-scratch over ground.
All I ask is that you turn to the child
inside, those words dreaming and changeless
as love's last chance—let them be said

against whatever, crying in the night,
we still think may be stopped, the black
historical fact of life's event
crashing, like a wall of water,
over the actuary's lawn and yours.

You have seen me before and would not hear, stung by your
wife's fierce beauty, when I called your name,
and the day your mother died I begged
your attention and got your dollar.
I followed you once, in New York, like truth,
always to give you the message, and now
on your porch, mud-spattered, I am
knocking to make you see what love is.
Call your wife, the police, anyone you like,

for everyone is waiting. We don't mean to be unkind but are
compelled to deliver, faithfully, the words
that have been fluttering in your ear
like a scream. It is not the wind
waking you, but the low roar of years
fumbling to tell you what has happened,
or will, when the door flies open
and the naked message of love
stands there stuttering in your face,
alive, crying, leaving nothing out.

for John Gardner

Goshawk, Antelope

Against snowpeaks, that country of blue sedge and shimmer
of distance rising into his tiny skull full of desire, he
fell across my windshield, a dot at sixty, and I, half-

looking for a place I had never seen, half-dreaming rooms
where blind miles of light lie on framed family faces,

saw him before he was anything, a spot above the glassy road
and in my eye, acetylene burned by brightness and hours
of passage. I saw memory. He came

out of the strange clouded horizon like the dark of whipped
phone wires and the quiet of first feathering shingles
in storm or in the hour of burial,

and dropped into absence where the antelope stood alive
at the fence of barbed wire, horns lifted slightly,
hovering on hooves' edge as if bored with the prospect
of leaps, long standing and still. The wind-

darted dust gave no image beyond itself, puffballs that turned
clockwise and counter-clockwise as he stood
changeless beneath that sudden whistle
of gray. I felt my heart

within those lovely shoulders flame and try to buck off
whatever the air had sent down as shapeless as obsession
and stopped my car, knowing already how
easily the talons dispossessed

all who, without illusions, lived. Dark and light bucked,
clung, shredded in me until I was again a boy on a fence,
hunched near the dream-contending world. But

someone far off was calling and I could not undream
what held me. Though I stood
at last it was late, too late. Someone
called and legs I had always trusted broke
but not in time and I fell from all chance
to change what was done or undone.

In Wyoming, in June, it was already starcold
though the mild blue of dusk beat back my mother's pain
when I saw him, small as a wind, shriek for the cliffs,
his dream gone, the aching wingless shoulders of the antelope
risen from a low mound of rocks, running from what was
unseen and there, like the red print of a hand

about to fall, for I was late and wishing to God for a tree
to hide under and see for once what had died
out of my life but would never leave or
come back as it had been—

like the slow growth of an antelope's legs into freedom
and away from desire's black whirling dream. It was
late, there had been no sign, no reason

to move except the call that might have been only dreamed,
but once I stood under the keening moon that, in Wyoming,
owns all that is and I begged the stars not to come
gouging my bitter and motherless sleep

where I lay long and longed, as I do now over barbed wire,
for the peace of the night-gleaming peaks and the flare
of absence that came, had fallen into

the accusing goshawk face of my father in that dark room
where I walked too late, where the glowing fur-tufts
of candle shadows drift on her face and his

and what was held has become, suddenly, lost like breath.

Under the Scrub Oak, a Red Shoe

Wrapped in a twisted brown stocking, strangled in the rolled
nylon of our grandmothers, it was wedged at the heart
of what little cool shade ever accumulated there.
You would have to walk out of your way, back
along an arroyo twisting and empty as memory, back
from the road out of town so far the sky itself
signals another world. To find it you do that,

though, in any case, you are simply walking and it appears,
something red shining through the gray-green glaze
of stunted limbs. If you were looking for a lost child,
your steps deliberate and slow, you might see it.
Otherwise you will go on. That is what we do.
But it waits to reveal itself, like an eye
in the darkness, and you may innocently look into that

moment, and may imagine why it lacks the slender heel which
must, once, have nailed many boys against a wall
where she walked. I kneel and pick it up
as you would, hearing though it is noon
the moony insects cry around her, hearing also
the nylon flake like pieces of skin against my skin,

feeling the sound of its passage from her shaven calf, a screech
like the hawk's when he is distant and not hungry.
In the arroyo no one could have seen her stop,
not as drunk as she pretended, sitting long
and, in time, methodically undressing, beyond
thinking now, placing her bundled shoe with care.
She must have been small and would have borne the usual

bruises, so we would have had no fear of any we might add,
when we stood smoking by the wall, catcalling lightly.
It would have been one of those nights the breath
aches it is so pleased with itself, then she

appeared in that red like the first cactus buds,
something clearly wrong with her but that, by God,
no concern of any red-blooded buck she might want.
In the junk car someone squealed, someone rose
and fell. There were no names. I did not mean

whatever I said, but said it because she was so small, she
could not hide her fear and shivered on her back.
Such moments we tell ourselves to walk away from,
and we do, as now I have walked in my hoping
for absence, but there is no absence, only
what waits, like this shoe, to reach, to say please
as best it can for whoever comes along, as if forgiveness
were what it meant, and love, as if any weather
that red shining endured was the bruise
you might have kissed and might not yet refuse.

The White Holster

Ribbed with red glitter, those glass studs catch
and hold the early lights my mother
has raised in her longing. Her
hands waist-high cradle my one
gift, lovingly, while behind
her shapeless black suit
the shragged green
of the little cedar hides
in the brilliant blinking of bulbs.
Out of the light, in the crooked
arm of the stairs, I wait and want
to enter the room where she is. I am

still a child, though already I know the meaning
of snow on the high hall window, that
incessant pecking like sand
the wind whips out of darkness,
piling it up until there is
no place and no time
except for the moment
glimpsed, as through glass,
deep inside the snow-wash.
This year the tiny Jesus hangs
in a matchbox and the tree
wears raveled strips of news-
paper bearing the names of the dead.
My naked feet slide on cold wood,
I feel my way down the dark,
for I do not want to hurry

to find her in the middle of that instant ice-
bright and all there will be of Christmas.
Long ago she called but I dawdled
in my bed to see how thin was
the white bulk of breath,

wanting and not wanting
to know how poor we had become
with a war raging and a father gone.
By each step I have grown larger
in her waiting, but am still
only a boy with no gift
except words

that, in memory, bristle and are evergreen as light
from a sparse bush she hacked and stood up
that night. I give them back now,
remembering how long it takes
to come into this loving

room where she stands for me,
her face, in sepia, slightly bent
over the white holster. The gun
suddenly silvers like a long stroke
of whirled snow before her body
and I see, now, she holds
my gift, the leather
stiff and white, the red tears
of glass, the black fake fur
in tufts making a pony's shape.
Her arms, light-bruised, extend

as if from the cedar's delicate, bent spine,
its fur and her dress one dark
blinking, as now my eyes open
and shut on that image. Words
fill that room with the rush
of needles gone crisp in time.
They sweep me into her arms,
words that lace the memory
of joy to the particular glint
of her hand on my hair. *It is
what you wanted isn't it? He said
in his last letter you would want it.*

Overhead tonight, in snowless December,
the stars blink quiet explosions.

Their bursts fall endlessly
on shoulders of rock and skirts
of cedar, until there is no square
inch of earth that does not gleam.
At stair top, with hand flat
on the wall, switch off now
so the tree squats alone,
I remember the long light
pooled on the floor,
that flesh and black suit
I must come down to.
All day I will draw guns,
deep in a child's joy,
shaking the cedar like a bomb.
Happy, I will shoot at her, *happy,*
until at last the words bang
from her mouth as she holds me,
saying *yes, yes, yes.*

The Collector of the Sun

Through the small door of a hut
he stares at us, our movements,
the thousands of faces we are,
the booming world's roar

that, later, for a drifting instant,
he will enter. His extra shirt
tied by its arms for a sack,
he will be lost in his luck.

By the freeway, whipped as a weed,
he stalks the malignant ground
for bottles, and we wear on.
He doesn't imagine anyone

weeping in anger as he looms up.
And when he comes to the truck
parked, the woman asleep inside,
he thinks of his nights, wide

as the blue glare on the concrete,
full of glass and the clink-clink
of his business. For him sunset
is the good hour, the shapeless

beams of headlights always thick,
blending with sun to flick
off what he hunts. He is alone,
himself, dreaming of the blown

treasures of the world, the bottles
like loaves of gold. The rubble
of everything falls about him
like snow. He bends, reaches, grins,

and ignores whatever we scream.
His tarpaper walls are the dream
he has given himself. At night
a wind plays over the pipes

he has fashioned from glassy mouths.
The world seems right, as he lies out
in bed, but fingers itch, and a face,
oh, whose is it, leans, leans like grace

and he can't remember whose or why.
At dawn, aching, he watches the sky,
sees dark birds pass, then us,
and is himself again, staring, blessed.

Rain Forest

The green mothering of moss knits shadow and light,
silence and call of each least bird where
we walk and find there are only a few words
we want to say: water, root, light, and love,
like the names of time. Stunned from ourselves
we are at tour's tail end, our guide long gone,
dawdling deep in what cannot be by any human
invented, a few square miles of the concentric
universe intricate as the whorls of fingertips.
The frailest twigs puff and flag in the giantism
of this elaborate grotto, and we are the dream,
before we know better, of an old grotesque
stonecutter who squats under a brow of sweat,
the afternoon a long glowing stalk of marble.
We have entered the huge inward drift behind
his eyes and wait to become ourselves. We stare
through limpid eyes into the vapor-lit past
where breath, wordlessly, like a near river
seams up, seams in and out and around darkness.
Somewhere far back in the hunch of shadows,
we stood by this wall of vines, and he, angry,
froze us in our tracks and the blade of belief.
That tree there bore the same long slithering
of light from a sky he owned. Disfigured now,
its trunk rises thick and black as a monument
that rings when struck. Here the hiking path,
a crease, stops, then spirals around into stumps.
Our party has gone that way, stumbling quietly.
From time to time, someone calls out but we know
only the words whispered from the wall of leaves:
water, root, light, and love. We stand silent
in the earliest air remembered, hearing at last
the distant and precise taps of the mallet
until our clothes, as if rotted, fall away
and the feckless light fixes us on the column

of our spines. Without warning, we begin to dance,
a bird cries, and another. Our feet seem to spark
on the hard dirt as we go round the black tree
and for no reason we know we see ourselves
throwing our heads back to laugh, our gums
and teeth shiny as cut wood, our eyes marbled,
straining to see where it comes from, that
hoarse rasp of joy, that clapping of hands
before which we may not speak or sing or ever stop.

In the Yard, Late Summer

In the yard the plum tree, wild
with a late summer wind,
shakes its thousand planets
of sweet flesh.
Does it mean to resist
this gush that drops
one order of things
into another? It keels,
leaning at forces we can't
see, can't know the edge of.
Its memory keeps only two
commands: this lives, this
dies from the licking sun.
There is no metaphor
to reveal what it has known
in its brooding years.
We watch the purple fruit fall
as leaves shear and snap
and nail themselves to light.
Between us the wind
is a word seeking a shape,
hovering in passion
and risen from the ground
of memory clenched
in roots and long tendrils.
Hearing that, knowing ourselves
wingless and bestial, we wait
for the sun to blow out,
for the return of that first
morning of pink blossoms
when we saw the dark stains
of our feet printing
what we were on that
dew-bed of the world.

The tree, too, waits
in its old unraveling
toward a naked silence,
its language wild and shocked.

Black Widow

I imagine her trying, trying to catch it. First,
dusting dutifully, but slowed by the child
leaning heavily under her dress, she finds
the web behind her hand loom. Her stalled
hands mean to weave a birth cloth, but surprise
her with another shape. On her face, the worst

black shadow crawls and squats and waits. In grace,
she bends, touches her loom to discovery.
The black spot hunches in the black heart
of the corner, snoozing in maternal revery.
Her hands now shake. The web gleams like art.
She feels her heaviness, her blood going to paste.

An hour watching steadies her pulse: she kneels
with the glass jar and makes an awkward strike.
Legs black as a satin dinner dress uncoil
and dance her back in memory to moves quick
in her body's dream. Clumsy, afraid, she fails
again—then succeeds, and screws tight the seal.

But punches a small hole for air. All afternoon
she keeps it in the freezer, admiring
that perfect beauty she cannot dispatch.
Home from work, the husband, I find the thing
dead I am supposed to kill. She won't watch.
In the yard the sun squeals. The sky bleeds blue.

We speak about small things, the future slips past.
She piles clothes in a discard box. I hold her,
driven to distance by the swollen bulb
of her womb, but she cries and shivers.
At night she wakes from a dreamed world
poisonously spinning, claiming her girlish waist

explodes, my foot on it like an executioner. She
swears she's full of spiders, still half
asleep, and kicks the blankets off to lie
naked in a little glow like an hourglass.
Accused, I roll in the sheets as if to hide
in my own dark the fear of what she bears and flees.

August, On the Rented Farm

In this season, through the clear tears
of discovery, my son calls me
to an abandoned barn. Among
spiders' goldspinning and the small
eulogies of crickets, he has entered
the showering secret of our lives,
and the light fur of something
half-eaten mats his hands.
Later, on a rotting length
of pine, we sit
under the star-brilliance
of birds fretting
the hollow light.
Under them, dreamless,
we have come to cast
our lot with songs
of celebration.
All afternoon we sit and become
lovers, his hand in mine
like a bird's delicate wing.
Everywhere the sparrows go down
to the river for the sweet
tears of communion. Soon,
in the yellow last light,
we will begin again to speak
of that light in the house
that is not ours, that is only
what we come to out of the fields
in the slow-plunging knowledge
of words trying to find a way home.

for Jeddie

Waving

In the backyard, by the stilled
oscillations of the cheap
metal fence defined
by the weight of children,
the small maple
waves in the first
gusts of a fall day.
Behind breath-frosted
glass, hearing far off
my child's cry, I
see this waving become
my father's thick arms.
He waves at the ball game
where players swarm
at his call. One spits.
He waves from the nose
of a rowboat, drunk
with fish, unashamed.
He waves at the black
end of a treeless street
where my mother has turned
from the house, crying.
He waves on a little hill
above the playground,
his whistle shearing
over each knuckle
of asphalt. When I stop
running, out of breath,
he is still there, waving,
and I am waving, beating
the air with my arms,
sore and afraid,
and there is no wind, only
the brilliant distance
like a fence between us,
waving and waving.

A Moment of Small Pillagers

That flock of starlings hewing the air
above the orchard is nothing
but the strangling of desire.
I know their country is nowhere
and would not throw a single stone
against such beautiful longing.
They have walked out to be
at the heart of our bodies,
and cannot find what they want,
or even a gleam from the gone sun.
Under them I bend down quietly
and pick up a black feather
as if it were the dropped scarf
of my sleeping daughter. Holding
this for hours, I find myself
unable to say a simple word
true or false, until I become
the little thing my body is
in the hiding fur of a woods.
Then I look across the hedgerows
at the foreign light of my house.
Somewhere in the distance of dark
a voice is calling my name,
but not too loud, and I want
to fly up and gather the last
radiance of the sun and take it
like a song down to her mouth.
Oh daughter, in the thick trees
where fruit bruises beyond joy,
I hunch among the starlings.

for Mary Catherine

The Dark Eyes of Daughters

Flying from the end of my
boot, my daughter's cat,
and the tame quail gone
up in a spatter of feathers,
to leave me turning there
as the dew dulls out, bare
shoulders flushed from that
quick sprint, the back door
still banging like a ripped
shred of memory. I think
I can hear the world grind.
I feel like a man in a car
who's just dropped something
to howl down a quiet street—
I am saying *Please, Please*
and only mean I want to go
on wherever I am going.
I want the trees to remain
a close, forgiving green
tunnel without that light
ahead banging down hard. I
do not want, for God's sake,
to hear this slow gouging
of sparks that the world is,
the intense unloosening stare
in the cat's eyes as I loom
out of the sudden stillness,
the fixed and believing
pupils of the child startled
to see what cruelty is, always
to know this first dream of
love's division. I am crying
Please, oh, Please—not
wanting this to happen yet,

sun the color of a cat falling
on her struck face that is
learning to mouth these words
without end, with only one
beginning already long lost
like pawprint or feather
where grass goes stunningly
dead and pain, like flint, strikes.

for Lael

Pine Cones

Any way you hold them, they hurt.
What's the use, then?

Once in our backyard, by a sparrow's hidden
tremor there in the green wish of spruce,
a full but unfolded body

hung. It bore every color of the world and was sweet
beyond measure. The canyon wind banged
at this then went elsewhere.

Something happened that night.
The sparrow seems to have seen what it was.

Look at him huddled there, mistakably some other shadow,
the sly outlines of his body almost blue as spruce,
the sun like a big wall nearby

and you stepping through it, big, that big
he would almost give up his only wish.

Almost. Almost. Almost.

Isn't this the way hearts beat in the world,
the way pine cones fall in the night
until they don't?

When you pick them up, as children do,
the tiny spot appears in your palm,
red as the sun's first blink
of love.

And that sticking unabidable tar.

A Gold of Birds

In Salt Lake City I saw an unremarkable sun
drop behind Antelope Island like a bloodstain
on snow, until the world festered red

and all night, lying in a dark room, felt on my skin
an unaccountable annoyance. The sheet on skin
lay acute, as with an extreme diabetic,
until I kicked it off and was naked
as a boy filling the room with his risen self,

but did not connect my jitters with sunset or bloodshed
and hardly understand any joining of eye and memory,
but know the grass everywhere had gone blood-bright
under a cloud-spattered blue sky and know

a swoop of birds cut a gold scar in what I saw, that silence,
where the world seemed no more than itself. The island
lay ridged against the boiling light but was
far west and only shadow in any case,
yet I strained to hear any sound there might be,

and heard the whipping of small wings. Then I saw the gold.
And saw one trailing bird shatter in the sudden scar
of the evening hawk that wheeled and went.
I saw wreckage drop into trees like black lake-stumps

and my body was rushing with excitement: I was a boy
walking home at dusk and my body smelled the girl
I had loved, finally, and there just over pines,
talons bloodied, he lifted as I came.

He did not flee, only circled to make his enormous cry
echo over the river long gold in the last light.
I went on into shadows and stood to see him drop

onto the darkened horizon, but saw nothing.
Except in the nightlong dream and sweat

of joy a face, in gold frame of hair, floated, fell away.
Her face, years now slipped under the heavy sheet,
gathered in what I thought was pain, but this
was only her dark secret, and is now

what I wake with, whispering for joy that kicks to be gold,
naked, silent as the first lips on your neck, gold
where what was blue goes red and bleeds itself empty.

Halloween Delight

Blue apple of the night,
apple of fear,
apple of peace,
the small leaves tear
and hiss in their fright
and the big moon screams

in its rut of the darkness.
Why is it hung there
on the starred rug
like a toy you hear
broken and distant? Why shrug
so? Have you not been blessed?

The boy who was once a man
thinks of no question
as he stands blued
by the dark that beckons.
He lifts his hand
and blots out the moon.

You have done this, long ago.
Perhaps you remember.
And recall that toy
now, and a night off far
watching apples as a boy.
They danced in the wind-blow.

Surely, you thought, by light
all will be torn.
And the leaves were, but
the apple held, shorn
as your heart's delight
nakedly crying where? why? what?

Only what is never answered,
nor ever is why.
Stand there and watch.
Small leaves rip and die
at home. Like love's speech.
Lift your hand, go on. Remember.

Reading the Books Our Children Have Written

They come into this room while the quail are crying to huddle up,
the canyon winds just beginning. They pass my big brown desk,
their faces damp and glistening as freshly washed peaches,
and offer themselves to be kissed. I am their father still.
I kiss them, I say *See you tomorrow!* Their light steps fade
down the stairs, what they are saying like the far stars
shrill, hard to understand. They are saying their father
writes his book and they are in it, for they are his loves.
Then they lie in their beds waiting for sleep, sometimes singing.

Later I get up and go down in darkness to find the hour they played
before they were scrubbed, before they brought me those faces.
There on the floor I find the stapled pages, the mildly strange
countenances of animals no one has ever seen, the tall man
who writes an endless story of those homeless in the night.
They have numbered every page and named each colorful wing.
They have done all this to surprise me, surprising themselves.
On the last lined yellow page, one has written: *This is a poem.*
Under this the other one's crayon answers: *See tomorrow!*

Pond

The soft forgiving ooze of the pond's bottom,
that cool fluid move through the toes
when you step out just beyond roots,
through weeds, into that black slough

that the dream has warned is love's terror:
to stand in this abiding rut among shells
born of ancestors, bearing the future,
is to feel all the flesh in the world

and to think of the last time you were in love,
the vertigo, the skidding infinite sky,
the lily's perfect, opening moves,
that slippery reek, that quick eternity.

Nekkid: Homage to Edgar Allan Poe

> Why was I there?
Fourteen, lank, moody, marked
by appetites that seeped up like convictions
in my parents, shipped off to summer camp near Richmond,

I wasn't Robbie or Bill, his drowned brother.
I would not launch myself stark *nekkid*
from the sycamore, however summer blistered,
however girls in canoes cheered
or welcome might be the hole
of the James.

I sucked in my Poe, suffered, at near anything flared,
thus was let alone, as weird.

Wearing black jeans, T-shirt, boots, beyond a rag-top Ford
parked by a syrupy creek, past an old wooden bridge
I climbed in my sweat along a path
that took me one morning clear

to a humped outcrop of bare stone with a view
of the valley, the river, and Poe's city.
> Below,
curves, mounds, the swelling distances straight down.

I edged out by inches, as if to the lip of truth,
daring death or fate, and bared my chest
and shouted at the depths.
Unanswered, I backed up, afraid of the fall,

but saw Richmond erect over its cobblestoned secrets.
From windows slaves framed in the air
the sun piked back
out of warehouses and wharves,
the prison, taverns, the sleeping rooms of whores,

so I imagined. Easy to believe
                              Poe came from this.
In my mind a manly city, state, what I wanted,
not this maze of green, long days with guides
droning the names of leaves.
What did I know of sap rising in the hard hollows?

I climbed because I wanted to *see,*
and not just the close-lapping slit
of the river you wallow from and never know.
I wanted to look at the whole spread-eagled beauty,
the thick pollution of foam
spit along the pink bumps and ridges,
the unknown tributaries and delicate archipelagos.

I knew that down there the boys went nekkid
and I would sometime, maybe.
                              Robbie's brother
told me it would be like swimming to the bottom,
your toes pushing from that muck,
eyes closed, trying to feel
your way headfirst to the air.
Then you'd scream and stink.

Climbing down with hunger to those I'd left bobbing
slick in the shallow pools, somewhere
from a socket of leaves
I heard it—
          that scoring wheeze of the flesh.
I stopped, uncertain, shadowed, still
hearing Robbie's brother's
words, maybe.
              The cry of this is the cry of that.

Her legs waved naked across his back.
As pale as I was, he buried himself in her
while I watched her face roll toward me and wink.
She grinned, whispered, while he plunged, near
enough I seemed to *feel* his shout:
                    "You dead son of a bitch."

I ran, certain this meant my throat cut,
busting through bush, my body ripping vines loose
that brought blood, and wasn't caught
unless you count nights lying awake, shaken, hoping
each rumor of footstep or leaf-fall meant
she had come to call me into darkness,

unless you count that appalling, grinning face
I carted home the summer I passed through Richmond,
a face as hopeless as the bridge I clattered over,
far more than nekkid
and deeper lost than Robbie's drowned brother.

Unless you count
the wishing I was not weird, not in love with her
wink, and not a son of a bitch
to be flung like spit into the universe.

The Soft Belly of the World

Probably in some vestigial ditch of the night,
flesh fevered, her crying finished,
she waits. Or has just gone
to buy the ticket to Tulsa,
by Greyhound and local carrier,
and does not think of the man who,
once, I was, the lean boy that fled
unscratched by the great stars
that scarcely notice us.
Probably she wept at seeing
the pure bright pearl of semen that dried
to a crust on the last stocking she owned.

How should a good girl go home, even where no home
is, legs naked, and wind ever cold?
Or maybe the enormous moon
howls through a window where
one yellow jonquil flakes
in her eyes and falls like a leaf
gold down the black well's throat,
that sudden and bottomless place.
It is her memory. The rain rings
but cannot wash away what happened
where a bucket hung and hands, the first,
went spidery under skirts lifted from her legs.

It might even be that she remembers nothing at all.
If the world forgets all we have done.
There is that chance. Her face boils
around the storm-staggered radio
where she lives. Maybe all she wants
is our manic country's heart
to forgive itself. This song
goes on trying to explain nakedness,
its lips drumming on the velvet

of her belly. It comes from Tulsa.
Her clothes, with her name sewn inside,
wait in supermarket bags, as she files herself.

All of her stories are true, and nobody's business.
She makes them up so she will know
she is real. But how can you tell
in the wind and the rain, alone?
The notes try to clatter through
and it seems she does not dream
but is dreamed by the jonquil.
Still as a lover's face it looks,
and she feels the root-knot
long to burst from its brown cage.
It will die, watered to death.
Why has she tried to keep it in the world?

Why has she, in this moment, had to rise up and go
to the window with its rivulets of faith?
Doll-placid, hair lank with rain,
she dressed herself at the sink.
The dress is silver lamé, like stars,
and will shimmer on the dirt road.
Now, with the last radio's
crackle, the room turns farmhouse
where naked feet sleepily shuffle.
At stair's landing, in a ticking pool,
she straps on her patent slippers
and begins to walk, head buried in the news.

Walks as if in dew and only to the deep well.
Dogwood made her skin pink and sweet.
She knows her name. Who else knows?
Maybe he is there, or will be soon,
who once sang her the sun and called
her Baby. Her hands fell down.
She couldn't know how furious love
might be in a person, how it
nailed on your lips those names
that weren't anyone's. She'd use them,
use whatever she had until it flaked dead,
and all softened again and time came to go home.

Portrait of a Lady

October, that glittering rakehell month,
snorts in the bushes where the widow is
busy with weeds. They still defeat her.
With them she has trafficked for years,
but what if she, puttering, with rake,
with shears, should suddenly discover
her fingers have gone numb? On knees
bent, face lifted so the black streaks
of earth seem time's batterings, she
may yet remember the high shrill stars
at the edge of summer and sing, for
behind them a darkness not earth parts
gently again and again. And if, then,
her brow in light sweat breaks to wear
the mask that runs to mud along bone,
let us lean close and watch and hear her
work as deep as ever through the hours.
She was beautiful once and may be again.
In October the leaves are lipped in ice
but heat, like hope, lingers in flowers,
under nails, in the cleaving song she sings.

Elk Ghosts: A Birth Memory

Tirelessly the stream licks the world until
from snow they do not come, but are
hoof-deep and standing, silhouettes
stark on the stones under stars.

Gathered, they seek a way to reenter
paths graven on the bone-walls.
Their white breath is alive. It is
possible to walk into and out

of monstrous, gentle eyes, knowing no link
exists except your face anchored
in the herd's dream. They are beyond
stillness and memory, their

revelation the lapping fire-fleck of water
and the starbright lintel of stones.
They come here to wait for change,
to be dreamed among pine and spruce.

There is no hawk who could hook them
out of the blue they breathe
effortlessly. Each moon-swollen
needle leads them more into vision.

Time conspires with you at night's window
and cannot help but hope for this
birth of joy. No longer do they
wait, no more nuzzle the future.

They glide through desire on earth.
Their thin song has entered each reed,
it has risen in your sleep and wails
forth these white shadows

you have summoned. They become electric
in your blood. One after another
they bear the stars, walking on water,
beasts with backs of pure light.

There is no world they cannot carry.
They are love's magi. Hooves flare
with a way through the darkness.
Composed, they suffer your coming.

Wedding Song

Camden, North Carolina, is not picturesque
though it is the place we remember
where many men and women have gone
in good luck and bad to repair
aching hearts: for five bucks
no one asks your age or looks for the curve

swelling under the skirt of the cheerleader.
Our justice of the peace pumped gas
and spoke the words through gums
long toothless and tobacco black.
A tourist honked for help.

He gave each of us a sample box of Cheer.
Y'all come on back anytime!

The first time down Route 17, by George Washington's
ditch, he of the chopped cherries,
we turned back in the Dismal Swamp.
Who could make up a truer thing than that?

You weren't fooling. Neither was I.

Believe this now: neither was I.
The second time we made it.

A wheezing clerk above an X-rated movie house
slowly printed our names.
He chewed an onion's golden rings.
He said, *Are you now or have you ever been crazy?*

Weren't we? Isn't love something that breaks,
drooling and dangling inside
like a car's hot-water hose
that leaves you helpless and godforsaken?

Y'all come on back anytime.
Fifty bucks and two economy boxes of Cheer—
how far could we get on that?

I was certain you'd end up croaking home
to mother after those early months.
Our first house had more holes
than we could cover, mice,
snakes, spiders, our dinner guests.

In that place you woke to the screams of a mare
who dropped half of her foal, dragging
half around our rented house
until with a tractor and chain
our landlord delivered us.

The chain still dangles in your dream,
and his *Y'all come back anytime.*

Sometimes when I think we have learned
to live in the world, the faces
of children lining our walls,
the darkness waiting ahead
like a swamp that's no joke,

I turn and find you coiled in a corner of light.
I think of the five green dollars unfurled
for that clerk of hunger and fools,
the blue acrid soap
that scoured us cherry red,
and the screams of our years.

Are we now or were we ever crazy?
Sign here, the man said, and we did,
the voices of men and women,
for love,
cracking up
through that black ancient floor.

I hear them still.

                    for Dee

Elegy in an Abandoned Boatyard

> *... mindful of the unhonored dead*
> —Thomas Gray

Here they stood, whom the Kecoughtan first believed
gods from another world, one pair of longjohns
each, bad-yellow, knotted with lice,
the godless bandy-legged runts
with ear bit off, or eye gouged,
       who killed and prayed
over whatever flew, squatted, or swam.

In huts hacked from mulberry, pine, and swamp cypress,
they huddled ripe as hounds.
At cockcrow scratched, shuffled paths,
took skiffs and ferried to dead-rise scows,
twenty-footers of local design and right draft
for oysters, crabs, and croakers.
      They were seaworthy.

According to diaries hand-scrawled, and terse court records,
our ancestors: barbarous, habitual, Virginians.

Some would not sail, came ashore, walked on the land,
kept faces clenched, lay seed and family,
moved often, and are gone. Of them
this harbor says nothing.
     Of the sea's workmen, not much,
no brass plate of honor, no monument in the square,
no square, merely the wreckage of a place.
       But they stood,
proud, surly in mist at the hovel of the boatwright,
the arm pointed: *Build me one like that yonder!*
Meaning the hull I see bottom up in ashen water—

nameless now as themselves, except to the squat one
known to crush clams in his palms, our kin,
the boatwright. He gave credit to each son,
barring feud, and took stick in hand

to dig from earth the grave first line of a keel,

who often would lift his brow seaward, but nothing said,
while a shape buried in air hove up
and he made it become what they wanted,
                              Like that one yonder!

And this was all the image for tomorrow he would give,
each reimagined, the best guess changing
to meet the sea's habitual story
of rot and stink and silence.
To make the hulls he knew
would riddle to nothing, he came
into this world as I have now entered his place
and sit at his charred and flood-finished log.

Only when I begin to hear the lies
he allowed each to invent
can I feel the hugeness of his belief, when I take up
a cap left as worthless, hung on a cypress stump, or feel
the plain cast of a stick pulse down my arm like the current
of conception—
                    then I see it,
                                 an immense shadow
on water.
                    My eyes harden,
                              and there it is,
                                         the wind cradle
of the Eagle's wings. As it might be for men,
even the least, riding the rising funnel
of air, dreaming change,
                              until I think of chicks screeching,
and the unborn who need us
to honor the places and the names of their passage
as we sit and try to dream back
the first wreckage, the last hope. I see
                              the one brother
become many floating and sinking,
lovely shadows all over the earth, and put my back
against the trunk they left me here, and pull
the stick to shape the dirt.

                    The line grows
quick with hunger, not perfect
but man-shaped and flight-worthy, a kind
of speech I take
for the unfinished country
the boatwright must have
dreamed, looking for his image
to rise and loom clearer
out of the water that beats in,
out of the water that bore us all here.

The Tire Hangs in the Yard

1.

First it was the secret place where I went to dream, end
of the childhood road, deep-tracked, the dark
behind my best friend's house, blackberry
thickets of darkness, and later
where we stared, with our girls, into the sky.

Past the hedgerow and the house-stolen field, past
the wing-shooting of crow remembered, I drive
bathed by green dashlight and the sun's
blood glinting on leaves just parted, then see

again the dead end, the dying woods, that stillness still
ticking like throat-rattle—and Jesus Christ
look at the beer cans, the traffic, even
hung on a berry vine somebody's rubber,

and wouldn't you know it that tire still hangs.

2.

In the Churchland Baptist Church the hot ivy hung, smelling
of dust, all mouths lifting their black holes
like a tire I kept dreaming. Clenched
by mother and father who stank sweetly in sweat,

I sang and sang until the black ceiling
of our house seemed to bellow with storm
and the tire skulled against my eyes
in time with the great clock in the far hall.

Hanging in darkness, like genitals, it made me listen.

3.

Years pass and memory's pendulum swings to changeless shame:
one summer night I came to fistfight Jim Jenrett,
whose house she came to and she no more now
than a frail hand on my cheek, and I
am beer-brave and nearly wild with all
the dozen piling from cars. Jesus,
look at us in the ghost-flare of headlights,
pissing, taunting, boy-shadows all right,
and me in the tire spinning my childish words.

We pass also, and are blind, into the years like trees
holding their scars, half-healed, the dark where Jim,
dunned by our words, goes out
near dawn and steps in the tire
and shies up the electric extension cord, noosed,
by the rope whose tire, burdened, ticks slowly.

4.

Ghost-heart of this place, of dreams, I give you a shove
and sure enough I hear the tick and all that was
is, and a girl straightening her skirt walks
smack against you and screams. You know
who laughs, smoking in the dark, don't you?

There are no headlights now, only the arc of blackness
gathering the hung world in its gullet. Blink
and maybe he's there, his great feet jammed
halfway in the hole of your heart,
gone halfway.

5.

Where do they go who once were with us on this dream road,
who flung themselves like seed under berry-
black nights, the faces black-clustered,
who could lean down and tell us
what love is and mercy and why now

I imagine a girl, mouth open in the sexual O, her hair
gone dull as soap scum, the husband grunting
as his fist smacks again, the scream
not out yet, nor the promise
she could never love anyone else.

I climb in the tire, swinging like a secret in the dark
woods surrounded by the homelights of strangers.
She swore she loved me best.

In the church I imagined this place left forever behind
but it's with me as I try to see the road begin.
Blackberries on both sides blackly hang.
Tall trees, in blackness, lean back at me.
When will they come, the headlights washing
over me like revelation, in cars
ticking and swirling?

Once when my mother could not find me, they came here.
Said "So this is it, the place." It was dark,
or nearly, and they said I might have died.
I asked them what being dead was like.
Like going blind or flying at night.

I shove my foot at the dirt and swing in absolute black.
The whine of the rope is like a distant scream.
I think, so this is it. Really it.

                                        for Robert Penn Warren

The Pornography Box

At eighteen, the U.S. Navy eye chart
memorized, reciting what was unseen,
my father enlisted for the duration.
At nineteen he caught a casual wave
wrong off Norfolk, our home, called
Hell by sailors. The landing craft
cast him loose and burst his knee.
He lived, and wore his rigid brace
without complaint, and never in his
life showed anyone his secret medal.
I stumbled into that brace and more
when I climbed to our sealed attic
the year a drunk blindsided him
to death in a ditch, and me to worse.

Today I watch my ten-year-old son race
over the slick pages of *Playboy,*
ashamed I brought it home, imagining
his unasked questions have answers.
I remember the chairs I stacked
and climbed, the brace I put on
to see how it felt and, buried
deep in his sea chest, the livid
shapes shoved so far in a slit
of darkness a man could reach them
only hunched, on all fours. I clawed
through families of discharged clothes,
ornaments for Christmas, to feel
the spooky silk of webs slickly
part on my face where blood rushed.

Trussed on their wide bed, my mother lay
surviving wreckage, stitched back
beyond the secrets I knew he kept.

I shimmied through a dark hole
in the ceiling and listened to pine
rake the roof like a man's shuffle.
But he was dead and the box unlocked.
His flashlight pulsed through my body,
each glossy pose burning my eyes
that knew only airbrush innocence.
Sex rose in me like a first beard.
A woman with painted nails peeled
a foreskin, another held a man
kingly rigid at her tongue's tip.
I could not catch my breath.

I blinked at one spread on a table covered
by lace grandmotherly clean and white.
Here might have been service for tea,
dainty cups, bread, a butter dish,
except she was in their place, clearly
young in middy suit. Behind her a vase
of daisies loomed, the parlor wall
held *Home, Sweet Home* in needlepoint,
and curtains were luminous at a window.
I remember the eyes, direct and flat,
as if she had died. Girlish stockings
knuckled at her knees, her plain skirt
neatly rolled. The man, in Victorian
suit, cradled her calves in furred hands,
and looked at the window, placid as
a navigator. He cut her like a knife.

After school, at night, weekend afternoons,
I raced to see them do it, legs cramped
in that freezing slot of darkness, gone
wobbly as a sailor into the country.
I came and went in the black tube,
ashamed, rooting like a hog to see.
In one sequence a black man held a pool
cue to a white woman, a black woman
held in both hands white and black balls.
The uniforms of sailors were scattered,
wadded everywhere I looked. I smelled

the mothballs from my father's chest
when late at night I woke to vomit
and stare at a clock's one-eyed glow.

How long does it go on, the throbbing dream,
waking obsessed with a hole in the air?
In Norfolk, from loaded cars, we spilled
at sailors passing alleys, asking where
we'd find some girls, beer, a good time.
All answers were sucker-punched. *Bye-Bye,
Seafood,* we screamed, then headed down
toward the Gaiety Theater and whores
bright as moths. We spit at mothers who
yelled *Fuck you, kid!* Crew-cut and clean,
the secrets of our fathers, we cruised
the hopeless streets shiny as razors
remembering nothing but naked images
whose neon flared like pus. Seeing now
my son bent to see I imagine at last

my father climbing before me in blackness,
with the tiny light a man carries, bent
on pained knees where I will kneel also
at nameless images we each live to love
and fear. One is a young Spanish dancer
whose crinolines flare out around her
hidden rose. Another cooks in high heels.
Among these are angels, blond sisters,
classmates suddenly gone from our towns,
one on a patio reclined, her long leg
crooked in invitation. She does not hide
the shorter leg. Each grins and burns
into our memory, speaking in shy whispers,
who are born to teach us violations.
At eighteen what fathers teach is wrong,
for the world is wrong, and only women
know why, their eyes dark and flat.

It isn't eyes that sons remember, blinded
by what never lies or leaves, but
sun's glint on that raw breast, that

thigh where face should not be but is,
and is the curve of the world's flesh
radiant in its rottenness, the secret
that leaves, finally apart and other,
all who walk on the earth. In memory
I see how each breast, each leg, each
face hissed our shame. By accident
I became the boy-father of the house,
owner of a family of obscenities.
What else is the world but a box,
false-bottomed, where the ugly truths
wait sailing in the skins of ancestors?

Escaping them at last I left for college.
But first climbed to what he left me,
carted that box and brace to grave,
and spilled those mild faces down
under the looming Baptist spire.
I spread gasoline where he lay, then
with his Navy Zippo snapped it off.
Quick bodies coiled and flamed, ash
flecks disappearing in sun forever.
I gouged the remains in a trench
of churchly dirt, tried once to spit,
then turned in the dark to catch a bus.
His pea-coat was black as the sea
at midnight but I took it and wore it,
sweating against the cold to come.

Women smiled as if I was ripe, flushed
with cash from months at sea. *Welcome,*
Anchor-Clanker. We've waited for you.
I was free, I thought, discharged from
Hell into the world that, for Christ's
sake, waited. I left home in a wink.
And would not go back at Christmas,
being after all busy, being holed up
with the nameless girl, the long blade
of her body even now slicing memory,
that darling who took my coat. But

by Easter was ready, went. House sold,
mother gone, maybe married, maybe Florida,
they said. I wandered in a cold sea-wind,
almost on shore leave, until I came
cast up where my father lay. Posters

of the nailed Jesus littered the grass,
announcing our inexplicable life. I saw
the crones kneeled there in sunbursts,
faceless, soft, as if to serve the sun
dying in the background. I shivered,
then rose up, hearing traffic hiss,
and walked until I found the old road.
I wished I had our goddamn stolen coat.
Boys yelled at me, but no one stopped.
Freed, I was myself. Who understands?
I walked hours in hard places, into night,
my first beard tingling, dreaming what
fathers know. Then came to a seedy hovel,
where films of flesh bared everything.
Among sailors I, a man, heard the siren
call us forward to sit with the darkness
under reels of lighted, loving women
in the theater called Art's House.
At love's edge, braced, we were nineteen.

So we went in.

The Colors of Our Age: Pink and Black

That year the war went on, nameless, somewhere,
but I felt no war in my heart,
not even the shotgun's ba-bam
at the brown blur of quail.
I abandoned brothers and fathers,
the slow march through marsh
and soybean nap where
at field's end the black shacks
noiselessly squatted under strings
of smoke. I wore flags of pink:
shirts, cuff links, belt, stitching.
Black pants noosed my ankles
into scuffed buck shoes.
I whistled Be-Bop-a-Lula
below a hat like Gene Vincent's.
My uniform for the light, and girls.

Or one girl, anyway, whose name I licked
like candy, for it was deliciously
pink as her sweater. Celia,
slow, drawling, and honey-haired,
whose lips hold in the deep mind
our malignant innocence of joy.
Among my children, on the first
of October, I sit for supper,
feet bare, tongue numb with smoke,
to help them sort out my history's
hysterical photographs. In pink
hands they take us up, fearless,
as we are funny and otherworldly.

Just beyond our sill two late hummingbirds,
black and white, fight for the feeder's
red, time-stalled one drop.
They dart in, drink, are gone,

and small hands part before me
an age of look-alikes, images
in time like a truce-wall
I stare over. The hot, warping
smell of concrete comes, fear
bitter as tear gas rakes
a public parking lot. Midtown
Shopping Center, Portsmouth, Va.,
the *Life* caption says, ink
faded only slightly, paper yellowing.

Everyone is here, centered, in horror
like Lee Oswald's stunned Ranger.
A 1958 Ford Victoria, finned,
top down and furred dice hung,
seems ready to leap in the background.
The black teenager, no name given,
glares at the lens in distraction.
Half-crouched, he shows no teeth,
is shirtless, finely muscled,
his arms extended like wings.
White sneakers with red stars
make him pigeon-toed, alert.
His fingers spread at his thighs
like Wilt Chamberlain trying
to know what moves and not look.

Three girls lean behind him, *Norcom H.S.*
stenciled on one who wears a circle
pin, another a ring and chain.
Their soft chocolate faces appear
glazed, cheeks like Almond Joys.
They face the other side, white,
reared the opposite direction,
barbered heads, ears, necks.
In between, a new shiny hammer
towers like an icon lifted
to its highest trajectory.
A Klan ring sinks into flesh,
third finger, left hand,
cuddling the hammer handle.

This man's shirt is white, soiled,
eagle-shaped, and voluminous. Collar up.
Each detail enters my eye like grit
from long nights without sleep.
I might have been this man, risen,
a small-town hero gone gimpy
with hatred of anyone's black eyes.
I watch the hummingbirds feint
and watch my children dismiss them,
focusing hammer and then a woman
tattooed under the man's scarred
and hairless forearm. The scroll
beneath the woman says *Freedom.*
Above her head, in dark letters
shaped like a school name on
my son's team jacket: *Seoul, 1954.*
When our youngest asks, I try
to answer: A soldier, a war . . .
"Was that black man the enemy?"

I watch the feeder's tiny eye-round
drop, perfect as a breast
under the sweater of a girl
I saw go down, scuttling
like a crab, low, hands no use
against whatever had come to beat
into her silky black curls.
Her eyes were like quick birds
when the hammer nailed
her boyfriend's skull. Sick,
she flew against Penney's wall,
our hands trying to slap her sane.
In the Smarte Shop, acidly,
the mannequins smiled
in disbelief. Then I was
yanked from the light, a door

opened. I fell, as in memory I fall
to a time before that time.
Celia and I had gone to a field,
blanket spread, church done,

no one to see, no one expected.
But the black shack door opened,
the man who'd been wordless,
always, spoke, his words intimate
as a brother's, but banging out.
He grinned, he laughed, he wouldn't
stop. I damned his lippy face
but too late. He wiggled
his way inside my head.
He looked out, kept looking
from car window, school mirror,
from face black and tongue
pink as the clothes he wore.

Often enough Celia shrieked for joy,
no place too strange or obscene
for her, a child of the South,
manic for the black inside.
When he fell, she squeezed
my hand and more, her lips came
fragrant at my ear. I see them
near my face, past the hammer.
But what do they say? Why, now,
do I feel the insuck of breath
as I begin to run—and from her?
Children, I lived there and wish
I could tell you this is only
a moment fading and long past.

But in Richmond, Charlotte, God knows
where else, by the ninth green,
at the end of a flagstone pathway
under pine shadow, a Buick waits
and I wait, heart hammering,
bearing the done and the undone,
unforgiven, wondering in what
year, in what terrible hour,
the summons will at last come.
That elegant card in the hand
below the seamless, sealed face—
when it calls whoever I am

will I stand for once and not run?
Or be whistled back, what I was, hers?

Out here, supper waiting, I watch my son
slip off, jacketed, time, place,
ancestors of no consequence to him,
no more than pictures a man carries
(unless a dunk-shot inscribed).
For him, we are the irrelevance of age.
Who, then, will tell him of wars,
of faces that gather in his face
like shadows? For Christ's sake
look, I call to him, or you will
have to wait, somewhere, with us.
There I am, nearest the stranger
whose hammer moves quicker
than the Lord's own hand. I am
only seventeen. I don't smoke.
That's my friend Celia, kissing me.
We don't know what we're doing.
We're wearing pink and black.
She's dead now, I think.

Cleaning a Fish

In her hand the knife, brisk, brilliant as moon-claw,
shaves the flesh. It grazes the white
belly just over the heart.
Underneath, the coiled fingers
are cradling a soft flesh
as if it were the jowls of the aged

man propped for a while on the bench in the park.
The head is not severed, the eyes not out.
Blue, they appear to flash odd ways
where a tree makes a live shadow.
Mostly the eyes are dead.
Nothing is in them

except the intense blue of sky the tree allows.
There is no conspiring of nerves,
no least event recalled
by a limb's high arching,
or even a girl's ascension
from a forgotten distance of water.

But there is something as she lifts the meat.
It is enough to draw down her gaze.
Now her arm rises against
yellow hair fallen
white in a childish face.
She is still as a leaf barely clinging.

I come to her like a cat in the stunned grass
and touch her to see the startled,
upthrusted gleam of her face.
At brow and each cheek
like gathered beads of mist
scales leap with the sun, and are dead.

No word passes between us, but something electric
as a flash of steel makes her
cry out just once. Squatting
at the yard's edge, she
sings beyond any thought.
Her knife flies as lethal as love
and cuts quickly in like a hurried kiss.

The Traveling Photographer: Circa 1880

Everything about him must be conjectured, his life
whatever a man's life is, succession of moments
under pine, catalpa, sedge, his sour
shirts, habitual horse, creaking wagon.

He takes no portraits of himself, on principle.
Yet, lying dreamless in the hot night, knows
it is all there, in plates
stacked, a joke no one learns the end of.

He laughs, and wind in the harness bell laughs.
Where, how did this life begin?
The plopping sound of the mare
makes him wish he could capture the night.

So much lost in black. He smells himself,
the heaving desert, and oddly
a wedge of butterscotch cake.
His mother, serving him, had laughed.
Son, go far. Dying.

Yes, *far*. The laugh, now,
burrs in his throat, but he remains
hungry, salivating at the ebb of his fire.

Closing his eyes, eyelids develop a cargo
of images (it is all there), the longing,
corn cakes, people, grubby people, their towns,
bluebonnet somewhere, stream, a snake weaving dust,
his wheels crossed it, the plate all
the evidence he was there.

Each thing is itself always, arcane
in the wagon, a junction without voice, theory, or
connection except the chuckhole's incessant clink-clink.

So little in all the world, monstrous
stars like a blacksmith's steel burning back the hoop
of his out-of-round wheels. The night trembles
like mountain water, aching his teeth.

Well, he will die soon enough.
He tries to remember an orchard at Shiloh,
sees instead the last plates stacked, is
nevertheless aware
his belly, too, prints the fishbone of his back.

Cat-squall, wolves, red-eye have been companions.
From the fire and from the glassy darkness
they leap like old friends. He is
somewhere west of Denver, mountains
black that had been green as fresh buffalo chips.

In dust before the trading post, patting his horse,
he had been ready to move on, had taken
all day two plates bartering.
The whore was not worth it.
The minister who repaired cabinets
fixed his wagon to shut as it ought to.

At his elbow the child's hand, the laboring breath.

They were waiting, still in the usual way.
He could not tell them from a thousand others scattered,
cinders of a prairie fire.

Father and mother centered, grandfather, sleeve pinned up,
children like stairs, too many.
Seat the smallest in the dirt, let them
have legs crossed.

Dead in the middle, in tiny coffin, the laced burden
upright against the sod door. Stitching,
fine red and green thread blossoms
on its tiny nightgown.

Color won't show, nor hours of work nor
the idle chatter before powder's explosions.
How did it happen? Name and age of the child? Well, God's

will be done. Wait for the wind
hotly swirling, and always long for a quick shot
of whiskey, for Christ's sake.
The nightgown had blown up, her flesh all sunk, sallow,
backbone, surely, clear as a fish in shale.
Made two more plates.

His father, the circuit rider, had condemned him
for those "damn pitchers" and burst himself
in clots on his mother's pillow.
Smoke from the campfire wavers like a face.

Had he had some kind of calling, a mission? What?
Night lowers itself at him again,
red-eye and the eerie blue of full moon.

At the stream's place, his image wobbles up at him.
The mare now and again lifts
its peaceable muzzle
to whicker whatever it whickers.

Things happen, things are. That's all.
Who has moved in the world more than he has,
gone farther, to know less?

Sometimes with his face splashed clean, flat on his back
between the stacked rows of glass plates,
the faces, unlost, try to speak.
He listens

until sleep comes, or dawn.
Sometimes their stories transform his own life,
strangers, nameless, become his father, his mother,
offering him children he calls Amelia and Darce.

Night-long they wheeze, electric as rattlesnake rattle.
Always with the first cluck to his horse

they are only themselves,
slabs of glass clinking behind him.

He has tried to be himself with poor luck.

Months into the wilderness, wheels busted again, fixed again,
pain like a broken tooth comes
in the middle of his chest.

Waking in the dead heat, his shop is cottonwood shade.
Late afternoon, the last plates prepared,
what does it matter?
Why hurry to have it all completed?

Works steadily, feeling fat, sore. Is it an illusion?

Held up to the sun, the glacial doll rivets him,
her eyes open, black holes gone red
as star-burn or wolves. Tilts it, then
again, and yes they had her
off-center, goddammit.

Sits down plop on the baked dirt, and stares. Stares,
then hurls the plate to shatter on dung-colored rocks.

"Longinus, we made mistakes but we tried."
The horse, at its name, blusters
head-down in witchy green.

The artist wakes dry-mouthed, unaware he had fallen asleep.
In late, brilliant sun, he lifts
the second plate close to his brow.
Head and body, he is rock-cradled.

The father, long-armed as an ape taken in Kansas City,
holds an apple hugely bitten.
He had not seen this.

Now sees. Squints,
lets it fall onto his face.

Feels the clench of his belly.
The seepage of saliva comes thickly.

Tries to spit, but cannot
force a thing to move, knows he is

hungry.
Eyes widening,
seeing as whole families do
into orange wolf-gleam of the sun,

he feels himself draining too quickly, blackness,
and fire sparks flying over ordinary ground
where all is ash, smoldering.

His wagon looms like one chance
for unity, brittle hope,
one last image

blurred,

near
and just so far.

for A.G., in memoriam

Wildfire

Crackling like fear in the child's heart late awakened,
the parents have gone into nightmare,
on the night lake of darkness
far away are carried, and the house
dreadfully closes.

It smiles like dawn in the wide western window.
No one believes this ever.
But there is glass-flutter.

There is wind hungering and the far sister
of the aspen trying to crawl.

Then it will be seen to leap the ridge distance,
going entirely.
Something has come in the dark, touching.
But the air wonderfully now

is sheepish and light lacquers all.

Snow-light nearly, down,
the singlet of geese travelers,
something like a word from the north,

this wholeness fully breathable
heaping its handful of gray on the ground.
Like mist and fog from a mill town rising
as if the earth had been just
created,

as it has,

and memory's hand opening above the coverlet,
and the family mouth open
and all over.

Dream Flight

Hawaii to Salt Lake City

Mid-January, leaving Honolulu, we are all tanned and strange
    with our secrets tucked away
under seats. Pillows spill from overhead. We lean into them,
    as into clouds, and safely
sail past Pearl Harbor, a submarine and wake clear below

but inexplicable as history or even our mute, cramped
    selves. Over coral and mild miles of
sea dreaming, I wonder how men and women survive and
    explain this world so vastly lavish.
Who are we, so constant in our going down, our rising up,

what news do we cart through the void above the cruising
    unbreakable shadow of our United
hunchback? We feel in its low roar we can climb above all,
    do, and light is shattering.
Many watch movies between worlds, but some glide in
    thought,

in the hiss of space where nothing is known except the
    selves who sit, exiles of speech, humps
of flesh and fear and hope, unable for a long time to alight.
    We see no streetlights, cars, roads,
no hills, no bowl of star-houses to remind us of anyone's life

in the home we dream. Great fish, down there, nose through
    whatever falls on a wind
of water. In their lives there is nothing unremembered or
    known. They go no place in love
or joy. If there is a shadow they enter it and become it

without fear, without knowledge that what they are always
    in is themselves, that harmony.

Dreaming of fish, I drift, I imagine the loved ones we fly to,
    the car that is waiting, soft
questions from runway to house. They do not want our
    secrets

exactly, only what we have bagged and brought back, gifts
    for children, what may be kept
from that other, illusory world. Coming home half asleep, I
    remember faces I have left,
and left before, their quick eyes in love with whatever rises

out of a place not even dreamed, a word only, like sunlight.
    Yet somehow I feel, floating,
I have become a bad gene they already harbor without
    knowing. Mid-sea, ungrounded, I see
the plane move backward to start over. Snow smothers the
    peaks

of Utah, home valleys dark as the volcano on the big island
    of Hawaii where I have not yet
gone. Houses sunk and dormant seem to erupt in the black.
    I stand at my child's window,
3 A.M., shadowy as a shark, from homelight about to fly far

over the black bottomland that once was ancient Lake
    Bonneville. Newspapers say the Salt Lake is
rising, the airport will go first, floodcrest only one, maybe
    two thousand years off. Our
houses will become the spewn gray mist. I feel in my body

bodiless ancestors claw to a rock under star-spillage. I see
    one who is speechless, a woman,
has just buried her children asleep in a mound of wool.
    Silver currents of breath eddy from
faces small by the fire. She squints into the heartquaking

ripple of wind. It makes her eyes water for a man absent,
    loved. Once he lifted her bonnet
by a pond and the sun flamingly poured. She felt herself
    charred. Now she wonders what he has
discovered down there in the salt-dark, blinks, shakes it off,

and tries, expressionlessly, to remember a day she pleased
      him. They breasted the snow. He
roared for delight. The white spume was like clouds. She
      feels unlike all others. Her prayer,
when it comes, comes wordless. It flickers from fire, star,

and spruce, from the orange head-crowns of children
      growing fast. It holds the land, unblooming where
below she will walk, flinging seed from her pocket. Hard
      ground waits unhoused like no-place.
Why, then, do tears glide? Does she feel she has slipped

under the far black plain of air? On the rock she sits ghostly.
      I, too, have stood and sat
in starless air, dizzied. I could not understand the enormous
      roar like selves disembodied.
And once at my child's window heard it, saw a doe's face

swimming toward me in the yard's snow, ice-legged, and I
      felt at my back some houselight
slowly spill into her knowing until she walked it and came
      near and knew me there, all secret.
I put my hand on sealed glass and hand-shadow fell into her

living so it lay upon her one great leap. I went with her, in
      dark. Among fliers head-cradled I
see how a moment of joy looks in and out, always untold,
      always known less than fully by anyone
who stands hard on the earth. But how say such a thing

and not turn the worm that night-long lies in the waiting
      hearts? In time we feel ourselves shaken,
bells ring, we strap our bodies down. We look in the dark
      for the place we must descend to.
So much pressure makes us believe we may not be the
      dreamed ones,

but, more than ever, we are. We remember what we have
      left behind, yet try to think of naming
the little we bring for those we bring ourselves back to. We
      say as we must, everything was just

as dreamed: trees with houses living in their limbs, fish

and fruit to be freely picked, bird song and a horizon
        brilliant as gold snow, a language of song
wonderful as natives whose skins stay honeyed in the mind,
        and rain pouring like prayer in its wild
surfeit on night-sleep. And from bags will come, like selves

promised, dresses of flowered silk, toys, figures slowly
        honed from the visions of a blind
Chinese father, a hand-carved unleaping deer, a chain of
        sweets, coral, snapshots of the black
self-sealed volcano. These ask no explanation and give none.

They unfold the fullness of themselves, they stand in our
        houses, on shelves, face up under stars.
They warn no one of anything, being dreamless, being only
        what shines in the light of the world,
sent down, as we are, into the black ancient lake of air.

Tide Pools

At dusk and long distance they are the mouths
to another world, caves of silence that speak
only in light, and tonight, family packed
for home travel, we take a last, slow route
over sand the sea has been all day cleaning.
At driftwood the children stop, first veering
off wordlessly, and kneel to know some texture
of change, or stand merely to dream themselves
freely into the gathering shadows of the land.
As we go ahead of them, we imagine their hands
collecting what seems to have waited for each,
shells, starfish, agates like a lover's eyes.
Then we also drift apart, each following deep
runnels the tide has left, and after a while
I see you hunched on a rock, almost part of it.

The light is nearly gone and the wind chills me
so I think of my father's whistle, ways it called
the sundered shadows of a family into the house.
But I do not whistle now, through the lips he made,
for somehow we have come where we may be apart
and whole. Instead I walk forward to understand
how each one is taken into the shapes of this place.

Then I find it, the deepest pool, rock-vaulted,
light bending and alive in water faintly moving.
I see the lacy deceptions, creatures disguised
as rock whose breath flutes in quick freshets.
A killdeer cries from the black suck of surf
and, though sweet, that darkness is not wanted.
This hole swells with the sun's last gold
and by it I learn to see what I always suspected—
the small, incessant pulsations of our lives.
For a while I stare into the spooling depth, and
here are bottomless eyes, open shells, a glitter

of hulls laid forever side by side like the dead
unwarily caught at last, perfect and untouchable.
How can I help sinking among those who loved us?

When finally I whistle there is almost no light,
but there's enough. You come then, invisible,
a sound made by the sand, a mingling of laughter,
and I duck under in time, holding my breath.
Eyes burning, I watch as you bend to find me.
How I love your squeal of delight when I burst
up like a king from underground! Soon we're all
in naked and splashing, flying up like white birds.
The road home will be long and dark, the stars cold,
but collected, like this, we will be buoyed beyond
the dark snags and splinters of what we once were.

Photographic Plate, Partly Spidered, Hampton
Roads, Virginia, with Model T Ford Mid-Channel

No one alive has seen such ice but the five-mile floor
of water so clenched itself salt broke down.
Among us even the age-wearied would not dream
you might walk the Chesapeake Bay
and look unafraid on its lucid darkness,

and the fathers of fathers, boatwrights, sailors of all
waters, never guessed this stuttering toy
might take them so far. But someone,
joking maybe, has rolled a small house
on perilous wheels down the banks
of the James, gunned it forward
for skids, runs, circles, a day
of such joyous noise the dead
seemed to have risen, so many
great-booted and black-coated are out there.

We cannot tell what they think, or if they find themselves
dancing on the road where no road ever was,
though there are long skirts, a few
thick-waisted grandmothers, even
a scatter of children cast about.
All of them are facing Norfolk,
where ships doze like unimaginable
beasts the sea has given to the dreams of men.

The Model T is small, black, plain, and appears
cornered like something risen through ice.
Hands reach in the hazed air
but do not touch what must be
chugging in a kind of terror.
The plate is dotted far and near.
Seagulls? Stains? Some mistake of glass?
And why do these faces look averted, cast down?

Among these is the one who will breed us, having crossed
a whiteness he will not speak about even to her
whose skirts he will shake us from.
But now gears spin inside him,
wheels, a future of machines. One day
he will tell my father he walked on water . . .
sick, chugging for breath, shunned as crazy,
who I remember by the habitual odor of gasoline.
When he died my father said he was too frightened to live.

Under the ice where they walk the dark is enormous.
All day I watch the backs turned away for the one face
that is mine, that is going to wheel at me the secrets of many.

Of Oystermen, Workboats

The wide, white, wing-boned washboards of twenty
footers, sloped, ridged to hold
a man's tongs and stride,
                      the good stance
to scrape deep with a motion like big applause,
plunging the teeth true beyond the known
mounds of the dead, the current carried
cloisters of murk,
                  miracles that bloom
luminous and unseen, sweet things to be
brought up, bejeweled, culled from husks,

as oystermen like odd angels glide far off enough
to keep a wake gentle as shirts on a line,
red baseball caps dipping like bloodied
heads upright, the clawed hand slapped
at the air in salute,
                    those washboards that splinter
the sun on tongs downlaid, on tines humming,

those womb-hulls harbored flank to flank at dusk
until the white-robed priest of the moon
stands tall to the sea's spume-pour
in nostrils
            of the men who sway from heel to heel,

the season come again, the socketed gray
of their eyes outward,
forearms naked past longjohns,
the salted breast-beaters at first light

lined up, ready to fly.

Smithfield Ham

Aged, bittersweet, in salt crusted, the pink meat
lined with the sun's flare, fissured
as a working man's skin at hat level,
I see far back the flesh fall
as the honed knife goes
through to the plate, the lost
voice saying ". . . it cuts easy as butter. . . ."

Brown sugar and grease tries to hold itself
still beneath the sawed knee's white.
Around the table the clatter of china
kept in the highboy echoes,
children squeal in a near room.

The hand sawing is grandfather's, knuckled,
steadily starting each naked plate
heaped when it ends. Mine
waits shyly to receive
under the tall ceiling
all aunts, uncles have gathered to hold.

My shirt white as the creased linen, I shine
before the wedge of cherry pie, coffee
black as the sugarless future.
My mother, proud in his glance,
whispers he has called for me and for ham.

Tonight I come back to eat in that house the sliced
muscle that fills me with an old thirst.
With each swallow, unslaked, I feel
his hand fall more upon mine,
that odd endless blessing
I cannot say the name of . . .
it comes again with her family

tale, the dead recalled, Depression,
the jobless, china sold, low sobs, sickness.

Chewing, I ask how he is. Close your mouth, she says.
This time, if he saw me, maybe he'd remember
himself, who thanklessly carved us
that cured meat. The Home has to
let us in, we've paid, maybe we
have to go. I gnaw a roll
left too long on the table.
When my knife screeches the plate,
my mother shakes her head, whining like a child.

Nothing's sharp anymore, I can't help it, she says.
Almost alone, I lift the scalded coffee
steeped black and bitter.
My mouth, as if incontinent,
dribbles and surprises us.
Her face is streaked with summer
dusk where katydids drill and die.

Wanting to tell her there's always tomorrow,
I say you're sunburned, beautiful as ever,
Gardening has put the smell of dirt on her.
Like a blade, her hand touches mine.
More? she whispers. Then, ". . . you think
you'll never get enough, so sweet,
until the swelling starts, the ache . . .
it's that thirst that wants
to bust a person open late at night."
I fill my cup again, drink, nod, listen.

Snow Owl

In snow veined with his blood and the white bruise
of a broken wing, the hiss in the mouth
salutes my hand and will have still
its pink plug of flesh.
Big as I am he would nail me
if only the legs lasted, those nubs
never made for this crawling, wings
that all night beat nowhere. He is himself. *Here*

Here, I cluck, on my knees edging toward him,
my own mastery the deceit of words.
His eye cocks, the hinged horn
of the beak tracks and rasps,
gathers its voice, shrills,
shrieks with a wind's rage . . .
the only language given to his kind

giving now his blunt answer to a world of pain.
I cast words on his white attention
like an ice he can't escape.
At each angle his bad wing
sends a storm of snow
between us, a blind conceit,
until I leave him, beaten,
who I never abandon in this life

of going home with flecked blood and snow's feather
on me like a shape I never have had.
Through the last spit of light,
trackless and numb, I go
limping until I cannot
stand, then lean on rock.
Out of this the moon rises.

All I know is this eye
long closed, holding
the world's unsayable secrets,
lifting and beating me onward.

Ducking: After Maupassant

You blew away, feather-brained for beauty.
　　Our gift is your sored blessing.

As when I was a child put down by my father
　　in the seal of sleep, I passed
　　　　under pines to an under-
belly of mists, and now I wait by our

duckpond's darkness. Here I lift my face
　　and the slender shotgun when
　　　　the sun rises to give me
models for the killing dream I have, ice

letting loose the cries I must learn to make.
　　You knew my kind, and the tolling
　　　　even in the mallard head
that like death's loud shock could not be

driven from any room where you lodged. Soon
　　flecked gold is going to be spilt
　　　　in this place, and I am one
hunched to kill whatever will leap before

the daylight entirely flaring. I am unchanged
　　by your sweet fable of fidelity
　　　　but think of a downed hen
and the drake you sent skidding into words

above her forever. Mostly you had to hope
　　Nature was not what you knew, or
　　　　more than that syphilitic
trail you left in the streets of Paris—

but all was, in the end, exactly as all seemed.
　　You lay wheezing and oozing, not

able even to imagine a face
that, being blind, you supplied from another.

And licked night's black bloodcrust from your lips.
  By first light screamed for paper,
    pen, a useless candle. Having
thrown open your blank eyes wide as a whore's

legs, a fable flowed. The maid wrote, then her
  scratching ended. Was it this way? Your
    door clanked shut like the shells
I have chambered already? In the far morning

then, perhaps, the hysteria of dogs, many crows.
  You had turned these to a bitter dream
    of ducks, thousands exploded
aloft that day you'd taken carriage and whore

for a cruise in the country. No one understood
  your pain, least of all her. Beautiful,
    she cried at the gunshot,
the gaudy cloud spiraling, and you slapped her.

How vile her cursing, yet inside you those words
  glowed, they were useful. A farmgirl,
    more than you she knew blood's
unreasonable purposes. Groaning, Ah, Monsieur,

she took your thrust after thrust while the time
  crusted in your head that would seep
    out black years later, enter
another's hands with your words, at one sitting

become everything you had to believe in or die. And
  died anyway, when done, stiffening to
    meat, and so much for Nature's
fabled fidelity. A madman dropped to the dirt.

Yet even as I lift my gun your dream rises, wind
  sifts the down of my hair. I remember

the knowledge it cost you, what
willingly you paid: the stories you forced out

of the whore, that ravaging of the flesh and blood
  for the last lie, for feathery dawn,

     our wordless father.

No Return Address

My son, gangly as the colts your family raised,
lolls around the table, then sniffs
at supper he barely eats before
he bolts to his room. He's saddled
with youth we had those boring Sundays
in church under tall pines years back.
Our girls are scattered in sleep as I
listen to the static rock surrounding
his lessons. He knows you only as
a name in the unimaginable place
where we began, a blurred idea.
I remember reading your awful scrawl.
It has got no better with time.

Five years, lumps that should have been run off
like too many potatoes, your letter names
our age, from Adidas to long laps
in therapeutic pools blue as memory,
an order of despair endured. You hiss
at treatments, sizzling rays, poison,
(". . . enough to kill *it*, not me . . ."),
those lies, we thought, in church—
when we thought at all. All swirls
abstract as a sermon in my head
trying to translate: you hired one
cabbie, black, to watch all night
the thing you'd become, motel
like a tomb he'd help you rise from,
wife, child in that bed miles off.
("If I died he'd know where to go,
what to do. I wanted them at home.")

How can I answer the news in these words?
Weather? Nights here are cold, they
horse at the windows. We're stalled,

we can't sneak out. Do you remember
your family's black Studebaker, the way
heroically we jumped from Sunday school
that May night, hot-wiring it? You
clutched, ground, unclutched,
hiccuped that hundred yards
to die under the caution light
at Casteen's Pure Oil? Casteen
like a giant shade in so much light
laughing, leaving us alone to push
our way in the darkness. Why? Old
as the world, that bastard was no help.

What were we that buggy summer, thirteen?
Jesus God, I'm as far from home as you,
uselessly trotting out sleek words
to keep a place alive with family.
You've done the same: the same tale
lied again, you and I caroming
in your father's hearse, nearly that,
to the bootlegger's lightless shack,
dogs snarling, a creek that stank,
me cringing while you nibbled out
our payments, laughed as black
as anyone who says I'm always here.
We've lived this lie so long it's
how we found the world we didn't know.
Your hobbled words still try to strut
with hope, looping and wobbling back
like women loved and nights of glory.
The truth is we had no fast phrases
for racy girls. We crawled by stones
in the churchyard, gagging on the worst,
pissing out the best we could dream.
The truth is we were alone, and are.

Wasn't that what Casteen meant to teach,
leaving us to snort God's heady words
of frail courage? That black cabbie,
hiring his kindness out all night,
drove you somewhere I can't find.

You were pale as a drunken boy.
He mailed your letter, not a word
of address or any home you've earned.
He's as invented as ancient Casteen,
sailing fares across a dark place
I can't guess. How can I explain
to my children all of us are thieves
he'll catch breathless as the brassy
gasp of words our parents stunned us with?
Young, we thought being alone meant
Sunday's boredom unrelieved, surrounded
by pews of kin. We leaped from them to be
together and alone. Now we are.

When my father died you broke the news.
Seventeen, huddled with a girl, I howled
at Jerry Lewis on the screen until
your blinking flashlight hooked me.
A shadow, you didn't speak. I listen
for the joke you might have made but
see that field of bobbing heads, still
black-mouthed and laughing as you
lead me through the aisle. It's Sunday
in May and we gallop to the hospital.
I should know where but don't. It rained,
and now rains here. I sit alone again.
I'm past the dead's age, diabetic, going
blind, tobacco-stained. Our parents say
it's too late to call. How can I reach you?
I go upstairs. Static fills my boy's room.

I snap it off. But rain gone to snow rasps
the window, makes me stand shadowing him
like dad. I've been watching local news,
the usual drunks, assaults, inexplicably
missing persons, a wash of words. Fronts
are moving in, silent days. The man
advises all of us to stay home if we can.
If not, he warns, keep shovels handy
for deep drifts, flares, drive with friends.
Reruns followed, then anthems, a luffing flag.

My boy, thirteen, breathes like the piney
place I've said we're going back to soon,
my lies becoming dreams we abandoned.
His homework, as always, is not yet done.
We'll wake snowed in. I kiss his forehead,
then for a while I watch a streetlight.
From here I can see it pulse in wind,
a message I don't understand. On and off.

for John Speers

Turn-of-the-Century House

The leaded, wiggly glass lives in its human length
as the squall, unpredicted, slams me down late
at night to see what in the world goes on wailing.
We have no lights. Lightning like a girl's grin
stands me dead center of the parlor. It's maples.

This house has its jitters yet. It's unreconstructed,
two claw-footed bathtubs, taps that won't turn off,
doors refusing their frames. Often they danced here.
Stars on the tin roof marked the place from near hills,

settling as thick as a shawl on a woman shaken awake.
It was only memory, but she woke her sisters anyway.
They stood on linoleum. Glass rattled and pipes clanged.
A bad storm, couldn't they see that? Ice, then snow.

The maples no one could bear cutting down, dangerous now,
raked the roof. Stars turned to ice, blinding the glass.
Can you see them, trying to sing as you would? Cold
swirls at the feet, dull yellow, naked as planked maple.
Water in the pipes forms red-streaked and pearl nails.

Your Christmas Present

This year we are sending you combs of honey
from Jaynes Farm, only six hard miles
west of the village where we live.
I have run with my body that far.
All summer I approached the apple trees
burning their best green light that
has now turned gold. We wish you
the green-gone-to-gold running of joy.
We wish you to remember the nights
long and black heaving star glitter
in the bees who ran on the hours of air,
giving the gift of themselves in gold.
We have wrapped this in local spruce
that it may smell clean and stay good.
We believe the wind sings us together.
Tonight our family is standing in the yard,
under the godly blue spruce, wearing
the magical light of the star mantle.
A long window light keeps our feet gold.
If you were here you would stand with us
to face Jaynes Farm where the bees wait
to work and the apple trees shiver again
and deer crane their necks upward, ghosts
who cross and recross the human road.
On your breads, when you come to eat,
squeeze the comb between your hands
so the gold runs out and gleams. Do not
consume the white husk or the green limbs,
else you may feel the coming of hooves
and the odd fanning of wings behind you.
Beyond this we have to advise everyone
there are gaping holes and you must
squeeze hard to think of us, filling them.

House Movers

Steadily down highways intractable roofs creep.
Whoever chooses them seems of one mind.
Sad white, pale green, the imagined result
of a going-out-of-business operation,
their clapboard hulls betray storied weather
by flaking paint and those stone-cracked
glasses just violated. Behind them steps
hang patiently, or a family porch waits
like a quick, amazed countryman. Required,
we think, are brute shoulders, blue jaws
and knuckles that gently graze a child's
face sliding under the edge of sleep.
These do not go with the houses, moored
families who seem alive only near pastures
where their fathers have lain for years.
Empty of each worn table and broken chair
used long nights to conjure, talk, puzzle,
the houses glide over our roads like veins,
ominous as we pass them and grip our wheels.
Wherever they arrive hard ground is gouged,
papers solemnly signed, lime is laid out,
the gray, bony, bite of foundations readied.
We imagine, driving sometimes behind them,
the black birdwings will start up, spiral,
a furred knob in the sumac will shudder,
clench itself down, and growl in its belly.
In a week no one will stop to feel suddenness
hunch unalterably there, like a growth,
or months after will remember what was
never so stingingly white. But shouldered
quietly at that rutted ground, our children
those first hours wait for children to pop out.
They lick their lips at the future come
as unlikely as death or birth among them.
Here, too, arrive the summoned around us,

from the tree-shrouded edges we live near,
the thick-thighed ones who pull and strike,
wielders of maul and nail and cold chain.
When we step in their tracks we become
the bare-soled children of their keeping.
We dance from their way, sidling, transfixed.
At night, our houses locked, we cannot guess
who chose how it would be. We lie under
the lipfall and spell of their hard songs.
In our heads walls ring, bow, and chant.

In the House of the Judge

All of them asleep, the suspiring everywhere is audible weight
   in the winter-shadowed house where I have dreamed
      night after night and stand now trying
  to believe it is only dust, no more than vent-spew
    risen from the idiotically huffing
grandfather of a furnace in the coal room's heart of darkness.

Haven't I touched the flesh-gray sift on bookshelves, on framed
   dim photographs of ancestors, on the clotted arms
      of the banjo clock that tolls past
  all resemblance to time and clicks like a musket's
steel hammer? And every day I wipe my glasses but still it comes,
  as now, at the top of the whining stairs, I am

come to wait with my hand laid light on the moon-slicked railing.
   I hear the house-heave of sleepers, and go jittery
      with no fear I can name. I feel myself
  shaped by the mica-fine motes that once were one
    body in earth until gouged, cracked,
left tumbled apart and scarcely glowing in a draft-fanned pit.

Pipes clank and gargle like years in the ashen veins of the Judge
   when they came to his house, the dung-heeled, some
      drunk, all with stuttered pleas to free
  their young, who could make it given a chance, just
one more good chance, so they said. Impassive, in skin-folds thick
  as a lizard, he stared at the great one for a sign,

the dog across the room, who kept a wary eye and was a one-man dog.
   Overhead do the same unbearable stars yet wheel
      in bright, ubiquitous malice, and what
  am I, wiping my glasses, certain this house walks
    in nail-clicking threat, going to plead?
I look out through warped Civil War glass buffed by men now ash

where the small park he gave in civic pride lies snow-blistered.
    Subzero then, as now, sent fire in the opening
        throat, but they came: tethered horses,
    striding shadows, and women who shrieked nightlong
until even gone they continued in his head. He heard them
breathing. He painted his house perfectly white.

I stare at that snow as at a scaffold. Whose lightening footprints
    could soften my fear or say why I sniff like a
        dog, seem to taste a skim of black air
    upsweeping the maple stairwell, and feel my hair
        go slowly white? How many hours must
a man watch snow shift the world before he sees it is only a dream

of useless hope stamped and restamped by the ash-steps of those we
    can do no justice to except in loving them? But
        what could he do before the raw facts
    of men cleaving flesh like boys hacking ice?
I think how he must have thought of his barking teacher of law:
    There is only truth and law! He had learned the law.

But what was the truth to leave him trembling like a child in prayer?
    In late years he kept the monster by his side, two shades
        walking alone in the ice, the nail-raker, one
    who howled without reason and clawed at the heart
        of door after door. In the end he was known
inseparable from his beast who, it was said, kept the Judge alive.

Until he was not. Until his house emptied. Until we came who I hear
    breathing, those heads warm as banked ash under my hand
        laid light as I have laid it on this railing.
    But are we only this upfloating and self-clinging ash
that loops freely through dark houses? Those enigmatic fissures
    I see circling the snow—are those only the tracks

of the dog I locked out, those black steps no more than a gleaming
    ice, or the face of some brother in the dirt betrayed,
        pleading, accusing? The moon, far off and dim,
    plays tricks with my eyes and the snow path turns dark as
a line of men marched into the earth. Whitely, my breath floats
    back at me, crying *I did not do this,* when the shuddering

courthouse clock across the square booms me back to myself. Dream's
    aftershock, the heirloom banjo starts to thud and drum
        so I turn and hustle downstairs to halt it.
    Even with my hands laid on its hands it wants to thump
        its malicious heart out, but I can do this
at least: I can hold on to help them sleep through another night.

I can sit for a while with love's ice-flickering darkness where ash
    is heavily filling my house. I can sit with my own
        nailed walker in the snow, one whistled
    under my hand without question or answer. If I sleep
he will pad the floors above the fire-pit. He will claw me awake
    to hear breathing in the still house of the Judge

            where I live.

False Spring: Late Snow

Everything in the village seemed to dance
all the dances of its kind all day long,
the whisk and pant of brooms early on,
doors slammed, dark gone to a green-gold,
the light ripeness of last leaves smoldering,
a hint of skunks on patrol, a cardinal's
ringing out the first gilt on thickened
limbs above yards, children in the streets,
from school, sweaters tied at waist, their
push and shove of shy courtship, squeals,
then the bronze houselights stepping out
from dinner, conversation low in wind

that startled me from reading, its absence
sudden as the winter's dead, the presences
who leave a house lightless, a chair empty.
Words stopped, seized like a rusted saw, as
snow buried us, eased us under, lost again.
I climbed the stairs, light-headed as a leaf,
to ride it out in dreams. I know it is
April, the blood-red bird home. A plow
grinds through winter's lie like the sun,
bumps, skitters, turns, making the earth
gleam black as the walls of a ballroom.
I think of two hand in hand, first sweet
steps into the swirling light, music coming.

Waking in the Endless Mountains

As if the stars were grinding audibly,
I wake scarcely an hour into the sleep
entered after watching a spring snow slick the road.
All night words stacked in my head remembering
until I believed once again the swirled
faces of the dead were calling.

The dog at my feet growled himself awake, shook, slept.
I climbed the tall stairs to bed and fell down.
Summoned, I do not know what startles
from me this need to walk out
bareheaded in the budding village,

but only a block off a fire is splitting the darkness.
Trucks with wide red lights wink and rumble.
A few men in black shrouds coil hoses
that seem to net the shining street.
Midway between this and my house

I begin to feel invisible as the blind buck
who stumbled in among us this winter.
Two or three watched him until a way out
opened his head. They led him
where our children cannot help,
though his legs will go on
breaking in their sleep.

When I look back at the room where I lived
leaf-shadow is flaring on her face
as she discovers I am gone.
The dog barks on the porch.

Nobody means to do this, to lie in the village dirt,
but the ground around me is cool, wet,

as if it is waiting like a mother
whispering many names.

All I want is to stand at the top of the stairs
once more, the hall light yellowing
the foreheads of those I love,
letting my voice be in their dreams,

saying softly, Goodbye. Goodbye.

Leaving Town

We left the town as we had come,
shyly, as a child speaks
to a patient waiting,
hardly noticed, traffic's hush
near, and elders remembering,
shaded by stoic oaks from noon.

We whistled down the cobblestones
we walked all the hours green
bloom was going brown, then back,
past new daylilies and the pond
where a small bear stood to see
what our smaller son did fishing.

We read the names on the park plaque,
no ancestors, but Union kin, and
hailed Sue's pigeons, the white dog
walking the Judge all winter. Fire
let the siren sleep, and the farmers.
Men worked at the courthouse clock.

Rivers we crossed seemed to race us
downhill. The high moon kept ahead,
coming on, ready we knew to find
us in the rooms above the stairs
we wouldn't be clattering anymore.
We couldn't shake it, fast as we drove.

We made a game. We would count, forget,
roll ahead like the numbers of miles.
The river multiplied and stayed.
Going south, dawn was a snowy fire.
Children fishing stopped to wave.
A man in a square marched on stone.

It was too odd to explain, and wrong,
as if all we had driven away from
said not so fast, and agreed
to travel in our tricks of words
and dreams of light, to be
with us in all the shapes we found.

Still we knew the time could not be
counted back, nor any town the same.
Daily we drove, singing roll us over,
till five lay down like the dead,
hoping we'd wake up at home,
desolate, afraid we were there.

Night Traffic Near Winchester

Through tall ash, through stunning cidery air,
under winesaps bobbing on every hill,
past leaf-littered fieldstone walls
mute as farmwomen bent in rows,
around weathered clapboard barns,
those veterans leaning casually,
quaint as postcards from the dark
drugstore that never closes,
catching the sour gargle of trucks
headed the other way, we descend

into the Valley, slow, ease our stop-and-go
route through painted brick cottages
huddled more than a century, and speak
of heartpine floors sloped so badly
no marble can hold its place here.
Like the hips of ancestors, each
foundation is cracked and patched,
still holding along the one-way
street that keeps the false yellow
farmhouse used by Stonewall Jackson
to plot raids dashing and thunderous
as the black Bible he slept with.
It's dark as a mapcase now, closed.

I promise we'll stop another time, stay
long enough to see boots, old orders,
the grim portraits like Puritan ghosts,
but now we climb, car straining until
we top the northern ridge and halt
where my father came year after year.
Stepping out, the crackle of leaves,
the chill, rare, high night drifts
me back to the smell of his coffee.

This is the way to grandmother's,
he says, so I say it now, feeling
this dark is my friend, a cliff
I seem to have lived under,
and below nothing's changed,
motors that howl all Friday night,
as if teamsters, hearing a rumor—
"Grant's passed Charlottesville"
—once more were beating
hell out of horses and boys. Only
it's just Route 17, the usual
grind toward home in the last hours.

Leaving the girls asleep in the car, my son,
old as I was with my father, steps off
to the overlook's lipfall I don't
need to see, all that historical dark,
and I come behind to take his hand.
His varsity jacket shines like a city
at Christmas, full of the thousands
of tiny lights we've climbed above,
yellow caution, white house, blue K-Mart,
and across a gulf of breath, that hill
steady with taillights like campfires.

Once I asked my father which army was
here and there those long nights, but
it didn't matter, he said, they were
men—any man's fire made a short
night when you were afraid. I'm afraid
at this edge the fathers have stood
before me. I pull at a hand that asks
"How far have we come?" I could say
I don't know, the usual evasion,
but over the lights, the dark road,
I hear the voice I had thought lost
say far, but not far enough yet.
Ahead, the family is sleeping, all
the lights on, coffee hot, ready for news.

Photograph of a Confederate Soldier Standing on Rocks in the James River at Richmond

A light rises,
falls, floats around the frame, a kind
of water swirling through generations
of years, pooling and shining when we look
at oblique corners, a given-back glimmer of one
come from a thatch of hickory heaving the home-field
still in his head, this boy turned in the sun's
stunned spilling where the river is
bristly as bayonets rippling,
                          one hung in light
like a leaf above that lipping darkness,
the hem of his greatcoat outflung.

                Why is he there? What man
in the war's middle stands like this with the teeth-
ragged remains of Richmond looming to the north?
We think he may dream of days the acorns
shelled down through yellow leaf-burst,
or mother's hand on him because in pools
the brackish bluegills would not
let him go home on time. Why
do we not think of a throat's thick fear?
Can fear be that shining on his face? Maybe
                         Fall's glory
that must be in each thread of the sorry homespun
he has taken through a toil of sun somehow
lets loose, leaves him alone. All his life
he remembers this walk, this stone-cradle turning
his face up to cliffs. We can almost see him think
not once can he say why he came, nor give any answer
for what in this split-second nails him forever
as no bullet could.
                Expressionless, he seeks us,
one-eyed, an eyepatch rampant over the left shoulder,

the right eye dark as a wound, and he cannot see
all the light in the world holds us to him,
all we are, the uncreated future,
                                        the image
which begins here as one apprehension
in the nerves of men, the secret
bond we almost know in that
instant we turn and lift ourselves
from the black river-roar and light-swarm.

Remembering Harpers Ferry

White, slope-shouldered, falling away in shade
as the land falls, windows half-shuttered,
odd glassy eyes in the cool morning of fogs.

The seam where each wind will howl is clear,
angles of slats still binding, scarred, the strain
of wood that's warped by bitter winters—who

lived here? we ask, slowing, imagining ourselves
in the cupola tilted like old hope. We stop
and trespass the slant of abandoned floors, steps,

furtive as a family in our talk of what's left.
Here the marriages, divorces, deaths of good wood
remain, mute beginnings, quaint in the snapshots

our children will box up in time: a rotten walk
we took, a tumbled foundation, ancestral hills
that keep heaving up wildflowers, planks, seams.

Winesaps

At dawn wind out of the north, hailflecks, pebbly
skates against windows. I lie thinking
the drainspout's drip comes
again in the basement
faucet where I am crying,
a child betrayed by death's
new cardinal and the cat
yawning on the porch
where my grandmother found me.

Risen now, I see the river full-bodied, its white
wind-knotted hair swirling like hers.
The polar hickory is naked
as a saber recalled by a girl
long gone in the gold
sauce of apples.
Two leaves that might be
cardinals returned
tumble in the hard light
at the brick fence.
Nothing moves in boxwood
where gray soldiers lie.

Among the last of them she walked, cupping apples,
staining her white frock, who took
a boy far back into the haze
the Shenandoah hills held
where family stallions
might walk aimless ground
littered with purpling flesh
beyond the cull of seasons.
Through a gate nailed
with leather belts
in my mind, I pass and enter
the arthritic orchard

tended by widows. What
I gather wakes me to think

how bright on the tongue was the taste kept
concealed, sustained, of flesh
abiding, months beneath
the wintering house floors.
To reach this I must go
down storm-worn stones
and pick my steps past
the sealed boxes of family
debris, nightgowns, flannels,
ribbons, birthspoons, a pair
of dulled skates, flowers
pressed in a moldy Bible.

Why is it we keep what we cannot bear
to use, and can't escape, shoving
ourselves into shrunken rooms
edged with old foolishness
unforgiven and unforgotten?
I fumble to the center
and pull a yellow light
down the ancient string
still dependably there
and stand, in my head,
as she did, playfully
asking where they went.
I know, I know, I say
back there in the dust
where I've come again
to look through tiny windows
into skirts of boxwood, a morning

that sends me alive among gray soldiers
at the house roots. I see also blue
preserving jars full of slick
pulpy flesh she has put up
in a juice thick as blood.
Behind it all in dark eaves,
baskets of apples, split

pine boxes like generations
steeping, undisturbed
by the tick and groan
of housepipes veining
the overhead I leave. Oh
let me see her light bring
back those stallion-feeders,
little red handfuls of joy! Look

how long I've slept, learning to walk
straight into a dawn-silvered web
where secret spiders spin
ceaseless as the seasons.
Above me ice takes each
room, I can hear feet
pacing fretful halls,
yet here I lift my face
and puff back all the silk
in the world. I hold every
core peeled on this slab.
My fingers claw the meat
of family stillness,
parting all the way to seeds.

Oh widows of the air,
fill me with your
cidery, useless lying,
those bladed hours
you fed me the dark
rotting dreams of your love.

An Antipastoral Memory of One Summer

It is written that a single hurricane holds the power
to run our whole country for one year. Imagine
lights in Minnesota chicken coops, firebells
ringing every borough of New York, dock pumps
spewing the bilge from Louisiana shrimpers,
the pulse that sends a voice from San Francisco
to Nagasaki where a woman wakes, folds, and refolds
the American edition of news already forgotten.

Yet even in the dark silos of our countrymen who
practice graceful moves at the missile's panel
that is like a piano with the amazing, unplayed
notes not even Beethoven could hear into fusion,
no one dreams how to harness the storm for good.
That is why I think of two people at a bulkhead,
an old woman desperately pushing down the hem
of her flowered dress, holding a boy's small hand
where the waves they have come to see blossom

one after another, sluicing over their driven hair,
the salt sting so strong their eyes begin to swell,
until they fall back across the elegant Boulevard,
and even there the unexpected crescendos boom in
laces and strings of water radiant as new light.
The noise is unforgettable and deafening, the sea
keeps orchestrating, as if it means to address
all our preparations, the boarded windows, the dead

cars with their rain-blistered glass, the sidewalk
clotted now with seaweed like abandoned bodies.
That suddenly, then, the calm eye stalls on them,
a stillness like a lock with no key, a hand
hovering at a switch, waiting for music unheard,

and see—the woman turns, drags the boy hard
past oaks older than them both, leaves this fall
blinking like lights, trembling, limbs like spears,
two entering a powerless house to huddle, to pray
to the still God, though they call it hurricane.

Ear Ache

The Great Depression sat on my grandfather
like Dante's Ugolino eating the malignancy
that betrayed him to insatiable hunger.
Left a lifelong fulminator at destiny,

he knew nothing he made or said would last.
My mother learned to ignore him, the hatred,
coarse cursing, and door-slamming at chance.
He played big-band trumpet in twenty-eight.

Then the country went bad and his ear broke
when the factories juked back to banging
work he had to take, grandmother's stroke.
The family saddled him with misery.

Yet he came one drab, silent night, hunched
over my body coiled in my stale bed,
growled about self-pity, and reached
to lay his scar-sizzled laborer's hand

at flesh that glowed like his cigarette.
The doctors had nodded over me for years—
"Maybe he'll grow out of it"—yet it
swelled back each winter, overwhelming cures

with sourceless pus. Penicillin, wonder drugs,
even radium needles shoved up my nose,
nothing worked. I'd lay limp as a rag
under books my mother stacked like stones,

their dulcet voices whining when I wanted
to jam my fingers in against the ache.
I see him bend close, that raw stunted
avatar of my line, his eyes slag-gray,

his ash piked coronal with deep inhaling.
The smoke he blows into my ear like words
stinks foul as the end of his welding's
spark-flurry, his skin scaling to blisters

while darkness crackles and he finds me there
crying that other day—"You'll go blind,
you little bastard, if you look at the fire,"
but it's in me already, the hammered bond

that rings in my ear unrecognized as courage.
The bubbling flux, the seams cooled, thickened,
his monstrous visor—I forget. Not the rage,
as he grips me, hurting, forcing this vision

to spiral back, the crooked stoop of a man,
nail-dirt, the smell of ash, smoke from the nose,
lips at my ear, sadness taking my hand
without hope, the song I hear him puff and blow.

The Family

In leaf green and brown vests, these shepherds
                of civility, hunters,
        stand in the sight of cousin and uncle,
echoes of words all that links me to them now
                when the night's sleet

gusts at my window, its shudder that thud of shot-
                guns over distant
        ground. My steaming coffee shows me
flushed from the wood's lip as I break to the cries
                they heave, words

triangulating to locate the home flight of doves
                down in impenetrable
        tangles of thorns and roots. I drop myself
into that stillness like the soul out of the sun,
                scrambling to hide

as the dove did, remembering their lessons, feathers
                of my skin pulled back
        to quick red, then I find it, a blink-
less husk I cradle and bring back in a man's too-big
                bag-coat. For this

I rose into the flesh-blue last light, the last
                time I was a boy
        disarmed and running, nearly one
of those who would stand while the tearing wings
                feathered fingers

with the little glue of blood, that papery ripping
                of breast so faint
        it was almost lost—but it stuck
in my head with the gut smell and weightless dance
                of tufts floating

like the gray breeze-riffled hair of my father. I
            see palm-sized
    bodies stripped on our kitchen's
counter, hear knives that click, the banging of
            the open breech,

smell the vanilla-sweet Hoppe's oil as I huddle at
                geometry's secrets
    while my father tells me I must try
to know more than the family has. This is the low
            moan of field talk—

guttural, innocent as love, half-understood under
            first seedburst of stars.
    When I brought them doves each would clap
an ungloved hand on my shoulder, breath would dart out
            in wing-rush until I

grew exhausted in this dream of manhood. Sometimes
            I hunched, unmoving,
    hidden in thickets as their pellets spent
through that trunk-world, ticking. They called me
            forth, the killers,

to blackness at field's edge, to feathery flesh-heaps.
            I would be silent,
    the smallest, learning to hear each cry
back "Night!" as he veered, and went, not knowing
            this wasn't goodbye,

was only the family name for whoever must stand last
            like a heartbeat
    left with its shadow, the father squinting
past numbers and kitchen glare, thermometer plunging
            to zero, one wisp

of feather stuck to the cheek I still kissed goodnight.
            Against black glass
    shining pellets of ice cluster, points
and melting lines urgent as faces hurling me to the ground
            of the abandoned,

and speechless bodies draining in the sink at dawn.
           Dark and nasty
   birds, in my head they are still as
beautiful as theorems, equations I cannot resolve
           to helpless answers.

Runaway

Someone in the supermarket cuffs his child,
a young man with his lip gray
from his first mustache, his arms filled
with bread, milk, eggs, the father muttering

              "You'll pay for this, double

maybe," and I hear anger's helplessness,
my father saying,
         "Go ahead. Be careful trouble
don't get you. Trouble likes a young boy."

His age now, I know he means a boy gone
in the world the first time, little
change in his pocket, hard days, curbstone
for pillow, if lucky. Nobody to bother

about beds unmade, or bitch over the uncut grass.
I see my mother bent in her chair, sun
twisting her brown curls. I never guessed
those hands at her waist held back any pain.

I watch the smoke at his fingers, a restless line
that won't break until ash tumbles.
               "When
you get there write, give us some sign
you're making it, whichever way you end up,"

the final words I think he spoke—but maybe
also
   "You sleep on things."
              Then nothing more
between us, except the night, and no one angry
for once, and her not screaming *Shut your face!*

Why is it sorrow I see, not anger? Hadn't I failed
my daily work, been churlish, hawked lies
he'd spit out with my name? Nailed
by his look, my mother follows him to bed.

Next day bacon, eggs, but not a single word
to stop me, and I want to ask about love
but can't as I eat in the light flared
through a dirty window. Dawn pays down the road.

I have come this far and I never asked him,
and he can't answer now. Except when
a boy I shout at trembles, his face a scrim
troubled by shadows, shouts, the words lashing back—
                              "Go ahead. Run."

Sawmill

The gold hill of woodchips at dawn huddles and sulks
like the hunched faces gathered to earn their way.
The young ones smoke, talk, and shake with the chill.

Up the clay road the thin-soled boots pull the others.
Cedar and plain pine thickens the air and two magpies
shriek, morning knives, until I remember the pulleys

cutting through sunbursts, dew-scald, and gears glazed
with red oil where skinned planks like bellies pass.
There a boy turns in his head to watch a girl's loose

skirt whip up in the night where he leaned. The banging
of big slabs dropped down shudders the soul already
closing its eyes against pain by noon. What can we say

about the hand not callused enough to resist beauty
of heartwood, the reacher we always miss too soon?
The blade, doe-freckled, that they call penis-cutter,

lies in its black bed as innocent as the serrated moon.
While there is still time, I spit, strut, dream of home
like a colt in the apple-dawn mists. Yet even so early

a siren slices around me, snatching all forward. The dark
boss moves among us, selecting his crew, naming a whore
so dangerous in our heads we laugh and forget the hours

we have stood when "another one got kissed." A cold sun
shoves through leaves hanging limp, breath of our women
in blue kneeling to blow fire into beds of little sticks.

Skating

I don't remember the precise shade
of gray along the oak's path,
or those long-lost
colorful characters fictitious
enough we might have made them up,
the girls that swooned
one after another
for the lips that jeered us.
This late I have to invent even
the gelatinous brown
at the clenched heart of the pond
where old bass finned,
heavy with scales
as the monks whose calloused hands
scratched back and forth
on vellum the assays
of the *Domesday Book,* that thicket
of causes and innuendo.
But over the ice, opaque as a cataract,
I moved, chugged, fell, and rose
like the great god of bass
trying to break down into a life,
until once I tripped on the slit
a good girl laid bare
as she flashed past in her skill.
Then the blood from my nose
steamed, it went out
like a small fire in a bed of snow.
Now I skate in words
for a moment of lips
flared under an oak with the speech
of mercy, causeless above me.

At parties, if there is a redheaded
woman, I bring along this story.

I take her to the corner
where the old music pools,
one with light like cream, my hands
cheeky with wine or whiskey.
I make it begin to snow, maybe
turn a road into a track.
I know she'll remember, too,
and she'll tell me
something with blood in it,
a tale round enough you can't find
its beginning or imagine
a reasonable end. The music is what keeps
us hanging together, in time
the slow beat changing
the light backward until we feel
a humming like water
grow hard enough to walk on, to shift
our feet and glide out
on the bristly first surface of being.
Suddenly we are nothing
save words, stories, hurtling beyond
all the others, in search
of that door through
the faces bloodlessly skating the room.
We say we are happy,
terribly, having no fear as we bend
into tomorrow's ice. Arm
in arm we swim under the gray towering
of an old crowd. While it lasts
we tell all the stories
from books dreamed about those who
fell and kept rising,
and others who watched, writing it down.

The Chesapeake and Ohio Canal

Thick now with sludge from the years of suburbs, with toys,
fenders, wine bottles, tampons, skeletons of possums,
edged by blankets of leaves, jellied wrappers unshakably
stuck to the scrub pines that somehow lift themselves
from the mossed wall of blockstone headlined a hundred
years back, this water is bruised as a shoe at Goodwill.
Its brown goes nowhere, neither does it remain, and elms
bend over its heavy back like patient fans, dreamlessly.
This is the death of hope's commerce, the death of cities
blank as winter light, the death of people who are gone
erratic and passive as summer's glittering water-skimmers.
Yet those two climbing that path like a single draft horse
saw the heart of the water break open only minutes ago,
and the rainbow trout walked its tail as if the evening
was only an offering in an unimaginable room where plans
inch ahead for the people, as if the trout always meant
to hang from their chain, to be borne through last shades
like a lure drawn carefully, deviously in the blue ache
of air that thickens still streets between brown walls.

Men Drafted

Downtown, in the Federal Building, a temple
thrown up by stone-loving governments
and the WPA fathers
long turned to dirt,
where once you could see
the people of the fields,
the tall ease of smoke,
and the river
they suffered,

we enter and peel ourselves
like new corn
among the white-coated
envoys officious
as those who bid blindly
on crop futures.
A shoed and shoeless line
of country skins,
we take up the position
on the tile floor,
waiting to be told
there is nothing
in our family darkness.

Each shuffles behind his brother
through barren rooms
the grave gray
of unknown utility.
Some pass without words,
having no hope
for the hillsides
they left, shaken down
here by the numbers.
Others joke richly,
their histories sealed

by the black marks
they come bearing
from family doctors.
We are all the same,

all of us covering ourselves
with fingers, some clipped,
some filth crusted,
keeping our heads mostly
down, as if spilling
seed in the rows
as mothers have taught us.
Station to station along
the yellow line,
we are needled, made
whole for the service
of death, culled
by codes we never know.

Under tall stone casements
we begin to feel pain
in the back, the knees
buckle, blood clots.
Shuffling, we grow still,
butted joint to joint
in long corridors
the fathers willed us.
Some, having seen at last
what's ahead, weep
softly, or go rigid
when the hammer falls
on the calf-face of the kneecap.

Hurting at last amber nightfall,
we find ourselves delivered
to piss, a wall grotesque
with crude dreams of boys
who will never come back.
One small window spends
a gruely light on all
the women drawn here as

in Bosch's *Garden of Delights*.
A sergeant shouts to press on.
I think of the painter's
aching arms, the smell of
flesh, women swollen, girls
ripening as they knelt
to hack the field down,
to raise it up again.

Leafless Trees, Chickahominy Swamp

Humorless, hundreds of trunks, gray in the blue expanse
where dusk leaves them hacked like a breastwork,
stripped like pikes planted to impale, the knots
of vines at each groin appearing placed by makers
schooled in grotesque campaigns. Mathew Brady's
plates show them as they are, the ageless stumps,
time-sanded solitaries, some clumped in squads
we might imagine veterans, except they're only wood,
and nothing in the world seems more dead than these.

Stopped by the lanes filled with homebound taillights,
we haven't seen the rumored Eagle we hoped to watch,
only a clutch of buzzards ferrying sticks for a nest.
Is this history, that we want the unchanged, useless
spines out there to thrust in our faces the human
qualities we covet? We read this place like generals
whose promised recruits don't show, unable to press on:
there is the languor of battle, troops who can't tell
themselves from the enemy, and file-hard fear gone

indifferent in the mortaring sun that will leave them
night after night standing in the same cold planes
of water. It never blooms or greens. It merely stinks.
Why can't we admit it's death, blameless, say that
festering scummy scene is nothing but a blown brainpan?
Why do we sit and sniff the rank hours keeping words
full of ground that only stares off our question: what
happened? Leaf-light in our heads, don't we mean why
these grisly emblems, the slime that won't swell to hope?

The rapacious odor of swamps all over the earth bubbles
sometimes to mist, fetid flesh we can't see but know
as cells composing, decomposing, illusions of the heart.
God knows what we'd do in there, we say, easing back
on the blacktop. Once we heard a whistling. Harmonicas?

But who'd listen? Surely all was green once, fragile
as a truce, words braiding sun and water, as on a lake
where families sang. What else would we hope for, do
in the dead miles nothing explains or changes or relieves?

Guinea Hens

They wait where the dirt lane unspools,
round and plump as mock oranges,
almost invisible in the black pines,
their thousands of pinched, hurt faces
all turning at once when I come home.
What have I forgotten that my wife
should seem to stand among these?
I lean on the wailing motorcycle,
a tide of whiskey in my head,
thinking there may be only one,
little heels like spurs, the shadow
of her wings sudden in the shaken
headlight I can't control. The night
ought to make me remember things
get tricky on a road like this,
the river's tongue luffing, the twin
red glow of eyes that watch, but
the world never helps a bit: it hides
each bump and rut, it summons one
bird to scream like the down-flung dead
in memory where bottles smirk. Lying
beside my love, I can see coming
home is the same pitched, lucky flight
into air the hen keeps. Black, sullen,
she waits with her grip on this place.
Whatever the world says, she's ready
to cackle, crow, rage, strut, and be
by morning soft in new light, nibbling.

Just Married

In the hammock, still white as a bridal gown,
the Father's Day gift, you feel the sun
fall through the first lacy outcroppings
of maple leaves, a hot green light
on your eyelids, and it's the same
easy floating you found her in that day
you woke inside her breath, pine sifting
audibly, the mockingbird playing his chords
over and over as if he knew you'd forget.

A life later, kids in school, no work today,
the bird sings, bringing back the service
performed by the justice of the peace, two
witnesses plucked from the sidewalk, and
now the little cries she made stir inside
your head where that green shadow drifts.
Awake, you slipped to the cottage window,
not wanting to be cruel, left her sleeping,
tugged on pants, strolled barefoot, hummed.

The pine cones hurt, but the river was cool
enough, so you walked, found the farmer
burying the spotted foal, sweat in his eyes.
Hunched on his fence you named your love
until he was done, until he spat and told
the story of the local doctor who never saw
a thing as the husband's knife slipped in
across the balls he was pumping with. Brown
teeth in the farmer's mouth gleamed then.
Your heart skittered like a small animal's.

Whatever love is, it is not a bird's song
you think as you feel the gray fingers
of clouds turn above you. Now you look up
where the mockingbird rasps on, ordinary

as the new moan of the hammock that means
only weight, change, the body that bends
around you, but not as she did, as light.
Now there's the sweat in the small cradle
of your back, the cruelty of crying out
the way you burst back on her, not caring
if anyone was with her, murderous, blank.

Skunked

Under the womb-heavy wheezing of spruce
she finds him and calls until he slides out,
that big unhousebroken baby we lost.
I watch from an eclipse of floodlights
my wife kneel and try to coax this dog
into a rubber bowl shaped to feed
a sow strong-jawed as death, but he
won't stay, he's racing in the darkness,
stinking up the leaves he goes through.
It's midnight when the sluicing begins,
and her crying. He's still out there
long after the tomato juice has turned
her bath pink as the dawn, after we've moved
two states away, after snow has sealed in
whatever expiations we gave ourselves.
Growing to be more than we could handle,
he won't return and we won't return.
We don't have pictures to show us
what happened. But when local dogs
howl like children, when thick summer
leaves us sleepless, oiled with sweat
like breast milk, I almost hear a snuffling
lift her and draw her out in her gown.
I see the red flow. I hear the spruce groan
over the first spurts like desire, then
something lets go and we're rooting
in the black yard, calling out names,
boiling water, then waiting as we must,
telling ourselves whatever we have to do
it won't hurt and it won't stink forever.

Reliable Heat

Delivers from distances of wood, dumptruck squalling,
a nation of red dirt wedged in its seams,
the hoist's screech a child
abandoned under big shirts flapping on a line.

Good mix, the black countryman says, stooped at his rig.
God's plenty of heat in that heavy log.
Feel it, meaning my wife, her
kind always tells, city or country, don't matter.

Stacking steadily, shirt off, brown as a pine, he's
a rooster at work, chattering a country's
need, lateborn mouths that wait.
I imagine the shadows he's cut in their place.

He warns me it's the hardheads hold out the longest,
wedged in like family. And sweetly keep the hearth blessed.

Pregnant

Think of the verbs by which they go: waddle, lumber, loll,
shudder, slide, shuffle, wander—
as if theirs is the aimless pulsing of summer-shallowed
streams through the mountain's
dreaming crowd of spruce. There the snake on his rock
lies conceiving a new self.
In the hot open meadows June bugs whirr and many cows
sway wide-mouthed, expectant.

Once in that grassy place, below the tall watch of the pine,
I laid my stained hand on you
most casually, and light as I could bear to be. All
particulars fall back to me
now, the humped, slight rippling I saw on a far hill,
wheat or weeds, a green shiver
of wind, something a man lost in the world can summon inside
if a far gone girl bumps near

just at dusk's edge when the groan of age is heavy upon him.
There was no dark yet with us and one
pool shuddered with the late day-flame, giving birth
to stones like small bright hopes.
Shoeless, you slipped in there, your skirt drawn up thighs
white as the growing mists
we'd come through, dawdling in ferns. I saw you show how
you'd dip a quick living thing out.

All these years leave me lying still on that barky bank,
sure I can hear the planet stop
to sing its praise of what you were under cloth's billowing.
Then water sang as the sun
shuffled off amazed. Now sometimes I see the hugely certain
gait, all trust, channeling down
city streets or through supermarkets, another of you come—
and your slow, lolling eye slides

upon me and I want once more to place my hand's shade where
you waddle with that quick weight
of the beginning, deliberate as the earth's dim intentions
you keep bearing like glory.
Let it be dusk, one bird crying, and already I am stirred,
my helpless touch uncoiling
with each of your firm goat-steps, my stranger's wide-eyed
face toothless, miraculously yours.

for Christina Nova

Stroke

All the long days of years lying
alone the word feels pelt of rain,
shivers of night chill, and coils
in the box you built. It whimpers.

At first light it stands, stretches
to leash-length, digs a small hole,
having learned to wait, become what
through all seasons and all faces

you can't say. Eye-brimming, recalling
the down-spiral of leaves, flushed
wingbeats and sun's joy, you lie flat
in the white yards of the clinic,

among victims low in tunnels of shade.
The word scratches, paces, softly
drags its chain over the emptied
bowl, barks. You can't call it now.

It won't hunt for you. Penned, you
wait and listen to machines digging
steadily as nails in dirt, a hole
regrettable, too deep, unfillable.

Chopping Wood

Strange how the mind will stand outside
the body's snapping torque and sweat
to observe bone and sinew that finds
almost never the perfect throw it wants

to split each round limb where the true
grain must expose itself, empurpled,
satiny as meat inside a beauty's thigh
stroked once in the permanent world

of love the mind summons only as smoke
or the wisps of breath in an iron air.
My body heat fogs my glasses, stroke
after stroke. The blade falls unaware

it might do anything else. Wood splits.
Most of it's knotted, and a worm hole,
hidden, is ubiquitous as tall innocence
the mind wants to bend to like a girl

impossibly gorgeous in a doctor's office.
And those hacking, impotent after-chops
at the hanging-on slivers?—they exhaust
caveats in the head. The fury of chips

flying up like prayers? Only the mind's
sad attempt to love what it must fear,
loose ground, bad aim, faithless hands.
So the mind heats itself with an hour

making fuel for heat: as if all consists
in the nerves hurling the mind out.
The blunt blade dives through the flesh
long dead, soon stacked, used up, mute.

De Soto

Tonight I am thinking of my lost cousin, the lights
of the city reaching toward me
over the black body of the river. They are almost
fingers, alive and cold, and one
cast down from the C&P telephone tower glows green
as the De Soto he drove, a wallowing
darkness with that fluid drive I remember he loved
roaring as we climbed cobblestones
past Aunt Dot's house. Her curtains were pulled in
against the afternoon, but we
weren't stopping that day, we were rolling for fun
at curves so the tires squealed
like scared pigs, me too, flung at the door he locked,
heading up to the high country
above Cumberland, just in time to see the Potomac
washing from red to a bleached
white while spirals of coal smoke stitched houses
shoulder to shoulder, a weave
wide as his arms. At the top he smoked and talked
of the Spaniard someone chose
to name our fat, sluggardly car. My cousin said that
great explorer had been buried,
a poor man like us, in the Mississippi River, and I
shivered, thinking of the dead
alone in the water bumping through endless coalyards
and sewers in the city I saw
pulsing at the bottom of the far dark—where maybe
Aunt Dot's husband was still
sunk in his chair at the parlor wall, his pipe's
plumes coiling through the dead
afternoon sun. I was seven or eight, at the homeplace
for the wake, that long day started
with the scrub of soap, learning to know scum
from the B&O can't be escaped.

In the garage I saw the wheezing tube that lifted
his De Soto like a boy
in a man's hand. He showed me how they put fingers
over oil lines for leaks
and we watched a man pump red ooze in each joint,
his eyes darting like Dot's
husband's when he bent near a diesel's big wheels.
Was it then I asked why
all the cars at Dot's small house, why my parents
wore black, why so much food?
I recall he swung me over the city and the river
he'd never let me fall down to
and I wanted to go home, fast, fearless, clenched
like a small black seed
inside the cushy wheeze of that car, my arms out-
spreading and unknown
as the tendrils in his lungs already, outrunning
the river, the laden body
of a freight grinding toward Pittsburgh where he
said we might go, sometime,
just exploring, and tonight I've come through there
bearing children who sleep.
It rains. There's little to think of, thinking of him,
mostly the mechanic's hands
at the steering wheel, highbeams on his face, a voice
telling me there's an edge
a man needs to keep to when he's coming down, tires
that hiss like family but hold
harder, longer than you'd ever guess, and you can go
a good way if you're ready.
Ready for what? I keep asking as I watch the river
snaking through hills, lights
of houses where people touch a child's face in bed.
What comes when thinking is over,
cousin, explorer? You winked and walked out on years
slippery as the road under me,
headed for the froth and swirl of the waiting waters,
your De Soto hunched and I'm
still waving from Dot's porch. I haven't yet entered
the parlor of smoking candles

where all the long dead are saying don't worry and I
won't know what they mean.
My first sip of our uncle's sweet wine doesn't flicker
in my stomach yet, no feeling
the road has just dropped away or risen back to greet
the body that floats in midair.

Field Music

At duskfall/haze layers each breast and cleft of hill
       flat as the dead's/combed/hair.
   I walk thick-tongued/my day's laboring
drowned by a tavern's glow of jukebox and cheap beer.
     In a nicking April wind/small criers
        huddled in weeds spring up,

surprised when I go from my road to theirs: a weed-way
       going down and back through
     the meadow's meazes like the unmade beds
of women in near factory shacks/widows whose spindly
     pension checks arrive small/and blue as
       the horned moon. Ahead/

below the ridge-brow/a portable radio beats out of earth.
      They wait, the same ghosts
    all these/years, two old garden-tenders,
ankles bruised with Spring's little smudge, knees runneled,
    the dead's woolen shirt drawn close to
      the flattened breasts. Heads

scarfed yellow as daffodils, like shy girls they dance,
      almost, shifting <u>foot</u> to f<u>oot</u>,
   talking softly over furrows, planting
done, between them snatches of song working to lift
    the bodies not risen away yet, words
      recalling labors,/loves

drifting off to nowhere, the field moon-whitened(as
      sheets abandoned in rooms
     faintly singing. By oncoming night un-
shaped/they sway together, darkly twinned, inexplicable
    wildflowers languid in thorned hedgerows
      of shadow. Why do they seem

to hurt my head with awe and longing? A pitiful vein of
                mist leg-deep is transforming
        whoever I am as I ease through a hollow
of hill-shade. Surely I can learn the language of fields
        for the touch of such does. But too soon
                I hear "Goodbye, love,"

and last muted steps, the electric pulse snaps off, leaves
                hiss underfoot, then a black
        truck ratcheting away, headlights skittery
as wild eyes cornered. Not far, then, I see them turn, stop,
        and I wait for something to draw me
                forward. Is it the door's

sprung banging that echoes so far in my brain? What
                perversion of need or
        hootch-fog makes me to stumble to seek
the ground they knelt at and held? Is this a vision
        of the Sublime: two night-scattered
                lunar girls? Why do I want

to know what their rough hands have offered? Running,
                I trip on the dark and fall
        down and tumble into grasses invisible
with swollen cocoons, milky snake-skins, a blossoming
        toad's belly-flesh, until I lie in
                a hard fetal amazement

seeming to hear them croon "Rise!" From the womb-wall
                of dirt I get up, furred
        by a dew-silken sheen, and I begin
slipping off shoes, clothes, imagining my skull gone
        burning with the claim of this place.
                I may be nothing more —

than blood-drunk, but something wolfish is in me, so I
                leap over the moon's fearful
        stream and slip through limbs like a smell
or a lunatic word every field wants, Loping past sighs
        of spruce, I think of the sleepless who
                stir, dreaming of anyone —

promised to return, the long hours of prayer to never be
        faithless. I am almost
    satyr and priest when at last I feel
myself stand down into the knee-ruts of crones who grapple
      this ground into blossom. Here I see
        in my head the one

face each ghost-breath spreads on the night window as she
      remembers the dead, wet
    shimmer of joy, I am out here waiting
like love, trying to find a way to keep these two forever
      humming the field music/of desire, but
        already, exhausted, they

turn to empty themselves for the laying down, small waters
      trickling into the darkness
    and the anonymous mists that swell
over each knot of flesh and hump of light. What can I
    do but howl, the spirit of a place
      bereft of angels or love?

I stand in the dark they worked, sing, let myself hang
      out of my body, making a splash
    that whispers all we are. This is the claim
we are going to return,/to stay, the oldest language. It
    gleams, taking moonlight's path to beauty,
      like breath, steady, blossoming.

(

Drag Race

Lying in bed I hear two come nose to nose
like fathers and sons, jockeying,
torque shaking the bodies
under the moonlight that shouts,
and the street goes instantly blacker
with rubber's balding death-howl
and the mind waking into panic
as if the house is exploding inside.
I smell the honeysuckle that accepts
again, as it must, the awful
drift of concussions, oil and smoke
snapping on houselights like fear
my father could never turn off.
Below, a boy's hand strikes the air
only, headlights lurch together,
locked to no horizon, wrestling
forth the veterans, also-rans of glory
who keep these crewcut lawns,
their faces shrouded in curtains
the war brides hung years ago.
I could rise and walk among them,
my fatherly robe star-silvered,
unthreading with age and forgiveness,
saying sleep, it won't happen again,
not the dog's territorial wail,
not the voices belligerently boyish,
not the beer bottle spidering sidewalks,
not my father swinging the night
back, hunching upright in my face
to snarl in the moonlight
I'm going to die in a scummy ditch
where love doesn't mean a damn thing.
I could call out *You!* to the boy
already hiding in the sweet vines,
certain they'll pick him up, sure

in his head he isn't alone.
I could put my hand on him like a tall
tracking shadow and make him
shiver this warm night, his mouth
outrageous as the arguments of power.
For each of us I could say it's over,
just the black street all that's left.
I might say go home now. We might
stand so close and still the others
would believe we were learning
the secret of living together—
the paralysis of place
terrible and silent as nightmares
with porchlights flaring on, off
inexplicable as tracers. But he
wouldn't listen, the light sheen
on him, holding like a fist.
Don't lie old man, he'd say, just
tell me what's going to happen.
Then I'd push him, tell him
get away punk, run, try to live,
each stunned throat of honeysuckle
understanding, nodding softly.

for Norman Dubie

James River Storm

The window's cracked against rain,
wind whistles inside, freshets
that clear the sky of smeared
clouds like ash on the hearth.
Yet strong that tang and thick
the dawn's damp as depression
bending the gray beard of grass.
Azaleas, tulips breast the field,
and jump like distant girls
but I watch one white-haired weed
flex in the fondle of gusts
where winter's last leaves
lie coiled awaiting the sun.

The crack of lightning has rattled off
to leave this stem burn in time
alone, its child-head silver go
thin and scatter seed and fall
to the vacantly waiting earth,
which is everything the river wants
in its night-surge and hunger.
But I let the river go on today,
and its cold, steady hush
like the high drone of a jet
over the Atlantic ferrying
so many glazed, draining faces.

Behind me you rise from another sleep,
your blood-button nipples sudden
as rain in the goblet of wine
we forgot. It, too, has waited
out the night, taken what it must,
steeped with what swells each cleft
and ditch and throat of wood
until the river's dark honey

seems a shimmering speech poised
at the lip-edge, unspeakable.
Soon the reckless heat of summer
will bake us still as the years
of conversations that lapse.

Naked on the edge of my chair, hands
clasping the sill wet as a lucky
branch above an eddy, I feel
this white crone effortlessly
turn to me, its wild milk still
loosing an inward flesh-shudder.
Along this river there are places
no man has seen, grottoes, aeries
of weed this one invites me to.
Each time I turn to you, nothing
has happened to drive me out
of my life, to make me forget
this storm-shimmered root of love.

Kitchen Windows

Because the house is too small, the season's
feast takes the living room
for its abundant lounge,
a great turkey sliced on the stereo,
bowls of jellied yams, stringbeans, jazzy
stuffing only steps away by plate.
On the table there's chicken,
amber as the last leaves where we park,
and ham singed black,
with toothpicked red ribbons, pineapple
moons like a child's eyes,
a coffee urn with its strong blessing.
Some kneel, some talk. Atop
the television is corn bread, swaddled rolls,
infants of butter, red sauces,
sugar white as snow not here yet, promised.
An old college trunk has preserves
with that odd, eerie sheen
turned bright where the television's on,
though no one watches
today's episode, the soap's family hacking
through the holiday fare
of sickness, betrayal, defeat, and the usual
edge of hope they leave
with the Grade B cleanser's scum rinsed shiny.
Somewhere there's three
kingly decanters of wine, all domestic.
I walk back through these
rooms to praise what happens to us all,
heaped meals we juggle on knees,
childish as clowns, boffo tales
we tell each on another, breaking to song,
loosening our collared,
formal loves, shifting from wine
to harder things, arms flung now to anyone

suddenly there like an oak
still golden in a world slipped graveyard gray.
How is it we always wind up
in the kitchen, hammy hips on stainless steel,
cheeks booze-ruddy again
that winter will wash pale, smoke hanging
like youth layer on layer,
our butts sizzled out in the sink? I stop
here, coat off, sleeves up,
tight as a tick in the warmth of friends,
laughing through sweat
on my neck. Soon I will slide out the side
door and stand in the blue
breathhook of nightfall, that sorrow come back
to be forgiven again.
I step to the cool edge of stones at the alley,
not myself, but some other
spirit, benign, from a far wood, and stand
lit up, glowing inside
that long, cast-out hope of kitchen light,
as Chaucer, leaving court,
stood before a gorged family tavern to think
the night enormous and bitter
for so many, yet shadows
already danced, ludicrously brave, and so happy.

Index of Titles

Index of First Lines

COPYRIGHT ACKNOWLEDGMENTS

I wish to express my sincere gratitude for grant support during the writing of these poems, especially to the American Academy and Institute of Arts and Letters, the John Simon Guggenheim Memorial Foundation, the National Endowment for the Arts, and the David P. Gardner Research Program of the University of Utah.

"Just Married" and "Skunked" originally appeared in *The American Poetry Review*.
  "The Family" and "Drag Race" originally appeared in *Antaeus*.
  "Skating" originally appeared in *Georgia Review*.
  "Sawmill" originally appeared in *The Iowa Review*.
  "Pregnant," "Field Music," and "Remembering Harpers Ferry" ("Ancestral Farmhouse") originally appeared in *The Kenyon Review*.
  "De Soto" originally appeared in *The Nation*.
  "James River Storm" and "Ear Ache" originally appeared in *New Republic*.
  The poems "Kitchen Windows," "An Antipastoral Memory of One Summer," "Chopping Wood," "Stroke," "Portrait of a Lady," and "Guinea Hens" originally appeared in *The New Yorker*.
  "Runaway" and "The Chesapeake and Ohio Canal" ("The Purpose of the Chesapeake & Ohio Canal") originally appeared in *Poetry*.
  "Winesaps" and "Men Drafted" were first published in the *Sewanee Review* 91 (Summer 1983).
  "On a Field Trip at Fredericksburg," "How to Get to Green Springs," "Cumberland Station," "The Spring Poem," "Night Fishing for Blues," "Boats" (originally published as two poems: "Looking for the Melungeon" and "The Cunner in the Calotype"), "Sailing the Back River," and "The Perspective & Limits of Snapshots" reprinted from *Cumberland Station*, by Dave Smith. Copyright © 1971, 1973, 1974, 1975, 1976 by Dave Smith. Reprinted by permission of the University of Illinois Press and *The New Yorker*. Some of the poems originally appeared in *The New Yorker*.
  "Messenger," "Goshawk, Antelope," "Under the Scrub Oak, A Red Shoe," "The White Holster," "The Collector of the Sun," "Rain Forest," "In the Yard, Late Summer," "Black Widow," "August, On the Rented Farm," "Waving," "A Moment of Small Pillagers," "The Dark Eyes of Daughters," "Pine Cones," and "A Gold of Birds" reprinted from *Goshawk, Antelope*, by Dave Smith, copyright © 1979 by Dave Smith, reprinted by permission of the University of Illinois Press and *The New Yorker*. Some of the poems originally appeared in *The New Yorker*.
  "Elegy in an Abandoned Boatyard," "The Tire Hangs in the Yard," "The Pornography Box," "The Colors of Our Age: Pink and Black," "Cleaning a Fish," "The Traveling Photographer: Circa 1880," "Wildfire," "Dream Flight," and "Tide Pools" reprinted from *Dream Flights*, by Dave Smith, copyright © 1981 by Dave Smith, reprinted by permission of the University of Illinois Press and *The New Yorker*. Some of the poems originally appeared in *The New Yorker*.

Grateful acknowledgment is made for permission to reprint:

  "Your Christmas Present": copyright © 1980 by Dave Smith; originally appeared in *The New Yorker*. "Turn-of-the-Century House": copyright © 1981 by Dave Smith; originally appeared in *The New Yorker*. "Photographic Plate, Partly Spidered, Hampton Roads, Virginia, with Model T Ford Mid-Channel," "Of Oystermen, Workboats,"